ADOPTIONLAND
from orphans to activists

ADOPTIONLAND
from orphans to activists

Curated by The Vance Twins

Edited by Janine Myung Ja, Michael Allen Potter, and Allen L. Vance

© 2014: Against Child Trafficking USA

All rights reserved. No part of this book may be reproduced without written permission of the contributors and/or editors, except in the case of quotations for articles and reviews.

Linoleum Block Image on Cover: Darius Morrison
Interior and Exterior Design: Vance Twins

Disclaimer: The purpose of this book is to give validation to families separated by adoption. Some names have been changed to maintain anonymity. The editors have been granted reprint permission from these authors.

ISBN: 9781500957940
ISBN-13: 978-1500957940

Dedication

This book is dedicated to Joseph Tae Holt (1952–1984) and Hyun-Su Kim (2011–2014) from South Korea and to Hana Alemu Befekadu Williams (1997–2011) from Ethiopia.

May they be remembered by the adoption community.

Acknowledgments

The Vance Twins would like to give special thanks to our contributors: Casper Andersen, Lily Arthur, Trace DeMeyer, Peter Dodds, Arun Dohle, Darelle Duncan, Erica Gehringer, Jeffrey Hancock, Bob Honecker, Cameron Horn, Tobias Hubinette, Sunny Jo Johnsen, Khara, Kristina Laine, Lakshmi, Tinan Leroy, Georgiana A. Macavei, Marion McMillan, Colette Noonan, Cryptic Omega, Vanessa Pearce, Michael Allen Potter, Paul Redmond, Lucy Sheen, Joe Soll, Daniel Ibn Zayd, and Darius Morrison.

Contents

Introduction   1

PART 1: *Saved*

Somebody Cares   5
Janine Myung Ja (South Korea-United States)

The Beginning of the End   15
Erica Gehringer (South Korea-United States)

Simply an American Now   23
Georgiana A. Macavei (Romania-United States)

Magnitude 7.3   29
Tinan Leroy (Haiti-France)

Nightmares Are Dreams, Too   37
Vanessa Pearce (India-Canada)

In Memory of Appa   43
Khara (South Korea-Norway)

Adoptee   49
Cryptic Omega (United States)

PART 2: *Unknown*

Letter from a Grounded New Yorker   53
Jeffrey Hancock (United States)

Without a Trace   57
Trace DeMeyer (United States)

Checking The Bastard Box   69
Michael Allen Potter (United States)

Outer Search/Inner Journey   77
Peter Dodds (Germany-United States)

What's It Like to Be "Adopted?"   81
Lucy Sheen (China-The United Kingdom)

Korean Drop   87
Sunny Jo Johnsen (South Korea-Norway)

Waiting for My Next Adoption   93
Bob Honecker (United States)

PART 3: *Abandoned*

Iron Bed 107
Darelle Duncan (Australia)

Immaculate Deceptions 109
Joe Soll (United States)

On Behalf of Scottish Mothers 119
Marion McMillan (Scotland)

My Inner Heart: From an Illiterate Birthmother 129
Lakshmi (India)

Fatherhood Stolen 133
Cameron Horn (Australia)

Our Stolen Son, Shane 151
Lily Arthur (Australia)

Bringing My Baby Home 165
Kristina Laine (United States)

PART 4: *Protected*

Stolen Lives 173
Colette Noonan (Australia)

My Son to My Rescue! 175
Jenette Vance (South Korea-United States)

Adoption: In the Best Interest of Whom? 181
Casper Andersen (India-Denmark)

A Critique of Intercountry Adoption 185
Tobias Hubinette (South Korea-Sweden)

Ireland's Banished Mothers 199
Paul Redmond (Ireland)

The New Abolition: Ending Adoption in Our Time 213
Daniel Ibn Zayd (Lebanon-United States)

I Can Never Forget 225
Arun Dohle (India-Germany)

Additional Resources 237
**Against Child Trafficking
Against Child Trafficking USA**

Introduction

"An awakened mother is a formidable force. She will not be railroaded. She will not be silenced." – Granny Alice Allen

WE ARE PROUD TO introduce a group of courageous individuals who have either been adopted or have lost a loved one to adoption. Most people, when they think of adoption, are concerned with the family that has been newly created. They tend to narrow the focus on the *adoptive* family. In the world of adoption, little attention has been given to the original family. If attention *is* given, the parent-child unit or the child's birth culture is usually presented through a disparaging and distrustful lens.

My twin and I were shocked to learn that adoption is not always *win-win* for all, like we had assumed while growing up. By recognizing the original family, it can be considered a *win-lose* situation. In fact, according to some families, adoption might even be seen as a *lose-lose* situation, on the part of the separated mother and child. Until 2004, my sister and I were only given one side of the adoption story. After digging under the surface, we noticed too many voices have been ignored. The problem is that those who have built the industry, and those who perpetuate it, tend to resist anyone who dares to question the happily-ever-after story that promotes the practice and validates the facilitator's agenda. This has caused parents (of adoption loss) and adult adopted people to feel unacknowledged and continuously devastated. Families of loss, and anyone who did not have the so-called *win-win* experience, deserve to be heard – *need to be heard* – if there is ever to be justice.

Still, some people believe we should only give voice to positive adoption stories.

We disagree.

There is courage at work in these narratives. We started this project hoping that it would highlight the strength of the human spirit.

We believe it has.

Many thanks to the contributors who generously shared their experiences and perspectives within the pages of this anthology. After reading each account, we were excited to learn that like-minded and like-hearted adopted people and first parents exist all over the world.

We are not alone.

And neither are you.

– **The Vance Twins**

PART 1: *Saved*

Somebody Cares

My Journey into Truth, Transparency, and Adoptionland

AS OF THIS WRITING, it has been ten years since my twin sister and I first traveled to Seoul, South Korea, to attend the 2004 Korean Adoptee Conference. It would also be the first time we intermingled with other Korean adoptees who had been sent to various Western nations. From the more than 160,000 children flown overseas by agency facilitators, 400 of us arrived in our motherland as adults intending to celebrate and contemplate fifty years of intercountry adoption. We made friends for life over the course of the trip. Like many others, we decided to use the opportunity to look for our Korean families.

My time in South Korea was the catalyst that led to a decade of research into the practice of intercountry adoption. I shared my initial thoughts and feelings inspired by the trip in a book titled *The Search for Mother Missing: A Peek Inside International Adoption*. It detailed how I became aware of emerging and divergent adoption perspectives.

The first surprise of the trip was when we discovered the street we were found on, according to the adoption documents, did not exist. *Was the street name a fabrication?* The "Certificate of Orphanhood" placed in our file gave the impression we were orphans, but could we still trust the accuracy of this paperwork? Later, we learned innumerable children were not actually orphans, but came from Korean families, families who would come back to the orphanages (or to the agencies) to retrieve their children. Because of the way the facilitators had set things up, however, Korean babies and children had already been flown overseas for profit.

Because we were not given satisfactory answers, numerous questions arose. Were we merely *manufactured* (or *paper*) *orphans* generated by lines of text? Were we labeled "orphans" in magazines and in advertising campaigns to make the transaction appear ethical? Even the definition of *orphan*, I later learned, had been manipulated to include children of single and/or "poor" parents. Did this allow facilitators to finagle more children from vulnerable parents? My sister and I were raised with the dogmatic belief that Korean babies were typically abandoned on street corners. Almost fifty years into the future, Korean-born adoptees are discovering that they actually came from loving families. My sister and I have also heard the adoption industry "targets children and abandons the mothers" (some mothers were merely given a bus ticket home in exchange for their babies). Weren't the mothers, then, the abandoned ones? And how many other mothers were treated with the same disregard? Is this a normal practice in Adoptionland? (And why is it still acceptable today?)

An "Unknown" Culture Club

During the 2004 Korean Adoptee Conference, intercountry adoptees could finally speak freely. Other situations occurred, but I did not grasp their significance until much later (due to my own self-doubt about my right to question the established industry). Fellow adult Korean adoptees, from their early twenties into their late fifties, confided in private sessions that they never stopped mourning the loss of their Korean families and were still trying to deal with the abuse and/or lack of care within their adoptive homes and communities. They were not joyfully relating fairytale endings or the type of stories regularly flaunted by the agencies. Many felt something seriously missing inside their loving, and not-so-loving, foreign (now adoptive) homes. Some relayed feeling rejected, lost between two worlds.

I listened to their stories and gave my own adoption some serious thought. The heartbreaking testimonials caught me by surprise. One thing we all had in common, it seemed, was that even though we had been sent to foreign families, we still also loved and appreciated them as our own. I had an added benefit. The close relationship that I shared with my twin sister prevented me from feeling deprived of my Korean family. Many agency employees had no qualms about separating siblings, even twins. It appeared as if expediting the shipment of children overseas had become the priority. We were lucky compared to siblings who were torn apart.

Korean adoptees were also upset by the lack of post-adoption services. I had even heard rumors that, in years past, agencies acted as a go-between to newly-reunited families. Employees would translate letters between mothers and adoptees (blacking out certain parts) to "protect" the adoptees or the "birth" mothers *from* each other.

I found out that it was common for agencies to claim we were "unwanted" babies while they convinced the mothers we (their children) did not want our "cosmopolitan" Western lives to be disturbed. This was untrue. After listening to numerous personal accounts, I learned suicide was one way that some adoptees escaped their unacknowledged trauma. In fact, Joseph Holt (an adopted "son" of the missionary farmers who set up the intercountry adoption system in South Korea), committed suicide in 1984 at the age of 32. Being severed from one's original family, culture, community, and country of birth was somehow "normalized" by way of adoption. Suspicions of abuse were to remain secret (even *from* the adoption community). One of the Holt's other Korean-born adopted "sons" drowned in 1972. What gave Harry and Bertha Holt the right to promise a "better" life to anyone sent to the United States when they so obviously turned a blind eye on the realities of adoption?

My adoptive mother adored the Holts, which, by extension, meant I also felt required to adore them. Questioning their work was the most difficult thing I have ever done.

At the adoptee conference, I cared about the other Korean adoptees, even seeing them as a community of soul sisters and brothers. When I heard that one adoptee threw an egg at one of the Holt's biological daughters (in frustration over his lack of access to his own birth records), I did not blame him one bit! I could totally see where he was coming from. Why should strangers be entitled to falsify our birth records? And why should they have more rights to our personal information than we do?

Another shock to my system was the fact that Korean parents were *looking* for their missing children. A Korean father even approached me in a back alley hoping to get help finding his missing son. One of the biggest problems with intercountry adoption is the language barrier. This begins when prospective couples fill out the application to adopt and then, because of the immense geographic distances, the imbalance continues throughout the course of the transaction. Transcultural adoptees are typically unable to communicate with their first families and often lack any contact with citizens from their countries of birth. This isolation can last a lifetime. These unfair economic advantages, working in tandem with the countless communication barriers, ensures there will be no "birth" family to contend with down the road for affluent couples wanting to adopt foreign children.

Being Called "Anti-Adoption"

Back home, I started to question the way babies were obtained for adoption. During the process of researching and writing, I tried to remain as neutral as possible and gave the adoption facilitators the benefit of the doubt (even giving them my trust) over the course of a full decade of reflection and study. I truly believed that they were saints and that I should respect them. They claimed that they were "saving" children, but their actions raised several red flags. As early as 1956, two years after they travelled to Seoul, the missionaries were already having trouble finding children, yet they were "swamped" with requests from Western couples (according to Bertha Holt's 1986 memoir, *Bring My Sons From Afar*). Soon, followers were scouring the Korean countryside for mothers who might be willing to relinquish their offspring. Bertha Holt's book revealed that some Korean children were "kicking and screaming" as they were pried from their mother's backs and that most Korean mothers sobbed as they waved goodbye to their sons and daughters, not understanding intercountry adoption, as it is known today, meant "a clean break and forever."

Eventually, these adoption pioneers were able to petition the governments to sanction the legal removal of children. In order to justify their activities, they claimed that they were "colorblind" and executing *God's will* (never considering God might actually be on the side of the splintered families). They set up the Child Welfare System in several countries. Those who investigated or protested at the time were demeaned and demonized. The name-calling continues today. The first label given to me was *orphan*, which enabled strangers to send me to foreigners, believing that this transfer was in my best interest. Forty years later, they call me "anti-adoption" (even though I love my adoptive family and they love me). This reactionary name-calling avoids the core issue involved: namely, the often unscrupulous methods used to harvest children for adoption.

If you continue to deconstruct the history of adoption while ruminating about your family, you might find yourself digging up more adoption irregularities, not because you want to, but because child trafficking is where adoption ultimately leads you. When I first started reading cases, I archived adoption articles online. At the time, I did not consider myself a writer (or a researcher), but rather a curious soul led by compassion and empathy for the families who were left behind. I had no idea about the grand scale of this industry or the missionary fervor involved with adoption. (I have since learned the practice is almost a religion to many!)

I started my investigations when I was very much pro-adoption. However, after learning about the myriad human rights violations involved, I could no longer advocate for a lucrative system predicated on a total disregard for the actual families it destroyed.

Today, adoption recruiters have targeted Africa's uncharted territory. In order to protect this continent from falling prey to child traffickers, officials around the world need to be educated about adoption trafficking. Safe havens from adoption brokers need to be set up within community centers, promising and promoting an agenda for the parent and child to be treated *as a unit* in order to protect vulnerable children from being sent off to foreign countries. Anti-adoption trafficking and children's rights curriculum needs to be taught at the university level by victims and survivors, not led by adoption facilitators or their allies. Also, for the past decade, Korean-born adoptees have discussed filing a suit against the facilitators who removed us from our origins with a complete disregard for our Korean parents and families (similar to Australia's "Stolen Generations," representing about 150,000 Aborigines, who were issued a national apology by the government on May 26th, 1998). I often wonder if my parents are languishing on the streets of South Korea right now. Is anyone looking after them?

Staying Neutral

While educating myself about adoption history, I remained on-the-fence and kept my mouth shut like a good little adoptee, eternally "grateful" and always "happy." I assumed that I had no right to voice an opinion on the issue, let alone to be openly critical of the thing itself. I remained a hermit, living in my own world, unknowingly imploding, dealing with my own trepidations and industry-induced shame about having the audacity to wonder about my Korean family when the industry dictated that I should remain loyal to my American guardians. I happily played the role for 40 years (and often still do). Reverting back to some of my roots, peaceful Eastern philosophies have comforted me through some difficult times in my adult life.

We have reached a time in history when adopted children (now adults) deserve consideration, especially those who were abused emotionally, mentally, physically, or sexually. Some authorities continue to fear that adoption is at risk of being abolished if we discuss things such as exactly *how* children are obtained or the reasoning behind altered and sealed birth certificates. The truth scares many people. Some might even be afraid of the collective voice of liberated adoptees. Some have yet to give themselves permission to see their own narratives through a wider lens.

The truth, conversely, has a way of liberating all of humanity. While we were growing up, we were told myths that caused trauma and pain. In order to become intact beings, however, we must investigate those lies. The truth might be difficult to acknowledge at first, but it is essential for humanity's evolution and for our own well-being.

If you were adopted, or are thinking about adopting, or if you have lost a child to adoption, you have a right to be informed about the way this man-made system has affected families globally. Please be aware and protect yourself! If you decide to be a messenger, you might be met with resistance or even fearful knee-jerk reactions. Friends might fear that, by discussing "negative" adoption stories, potential adopters might be dissuaded from adopting. You might be told not to rock the boat, to remain positive, to stop being "bitter," and to only relay successful adoption stories. However, you have a right to voice concerns. For years, investigative journalists have been reporting that children have been kidnapped for adoption, yet still, no laws have been passed to protect families from this type of atrocity. It is imperative that those of us in the adoptee community address the problem before more babies and young children are falsely tagged as "orphans" and unnecessarily placed into the arms of strangers.

Within the confines of adoption culture, adopted people are not supposed to know about their roots. Facilitators have expected us to smile for the camera, to be grateful, and not to ask too many questions. It is now being recognized that all humans deserve to have access to their individual origins and should have a right to share their perspectives (even if they disagree with the predominate thinking).

"Nobody cares," we were told by those on the profitable side of the fence. Sometimes it may seem as if no one cares.

People do care.

Some adoptive parents might have a hard time accepting these findings at first, but there is reason for optimism. It actually took our own adoptive father a short time to understand that the hidden side of adoption had yet to be spoken, seen, or heard and that these omissions actively contribute to the perpetuation of abuse.

The trouble with painting *all* adoptions as good—which is the North American presumption—is that those who have been obtained fraudulently (namely, trafficked) are ignored and, therefore, refused due consideration and reconciliation. Someone needed to admit that adoption is not always a "win-win" on both sides of the equation, as it is endorsed in agency marketing campaigns. Adult adopted people must be cautious of the way facilitators will, finally, invite us into the adoption industry arena by tempting us with a salary to promote "better" practices. We might be so elated at the invitation that our emotions will not allow us to see the toxic buffet. Years of adoption propaganda have fueled the seemingly insatiable demand for children. To the exploited families and their missing children (now adults) still without answers and access to health history and ancestry, adoption can no longer be considered "in the best interest of the child." Not when adoption means children are being "legally" trafficked for profit.

At first, it appeared no one cared. Then, in 2011, my sister and I co-founded a group called "The Adoption Truth and Transparency Worldwide Network." Hundreds of exceptional individuals, mostly parents who had lost their children to adoption, started joining our group. We started getting private messages from parents who appreciated being heard. To date, more than 5,000 people have joined this community. Some are from splintered families and others are hardworking adoptee-rights activists. Some feel acknowledged for the very first time and others have been coping with the pain of adoption for many years, even decades. More needs to be done to create safe spaces for discussion and healing.

Those who seek truth and transparency do not represent the dark side of adoption, but rather, a beacon of hope in the midst of an imperfect, unregulated, and incredibly profitable industry. Once we heard the true stories, as opposed to the rhetoric from the agencies, we knew our efforts to spread awareness were well worth the struggle. We have been fortunate to find an organization that has been fighting for the rights of parents who have lost their children to adoption trafficking. Against Child Trafficking is conducting necessary research and investigational fieldwork.

It has been almost ten years since my trip to South Korea. I have learned that some segment of the public might not care about first families, but we do. For every family created by adoption, another family exists that has been forever torn apart, either across the street or across the globe.

Since my sister and I started listening, we have heard thousands of stories that mirror our initial feelings of doubt and uncertainty. Now the voices of first families have become a chorus of validation. Adopted people started joining our group and now they have a space to educate the public on unfamiliar insights into the practice. These courageous and assertive individuals are willing to see adoption through a wider lens, which includes the experiences of families from around the world. The social media group has provided a platform for open discussions, oftentimes uncomfortable, essential to someday protecting families from being unnecessarily separated. I have written about adoption to the best of my ability, but I have found *listening* is the best way to show I care.

This is the journey that led me into truth, transparency, and *Adoptionland*.

Janine Myung Ja is the author of *Twins Found in a Box: Adapting to Adoption, The Search for Mother Missing: A Peek Inside Intercountry Adoption*, and co-editor of *The "Unknown" Culture Club: Korean Adoptees, Then and Now*, an anthology that serves as a tribute for transracially adopted people (particularly from Asia). She has also written several feature-length screenplays on the transnational adoption experience. She is the co-creator of the social media group "Adoption Truth and Transparency Worldwide Network" and is a supporter of Against Child Trafficking's investigational work into unethical adoptions. Her passions include metaphysics, philosophy, spirit writing, and meditation. You can find Janine online at: *Adoptionland.org* and *Adoptionhistory101.com*.

The Beginning of the End

WITH NO LESS THAN six cups of coffee in my stomach at the Asian-American conference hosted at the University of Michigan, I felt as though I was lost in a sea of my own ancestry. Everywhere I looked, there seemed to be some sort of ethnic person who shared the same yellow skin as me, but I still felt as if I truly didn't belong. *Why not?* I kept thinking, *If we all looked alike, didn't that mean we could automatically connect with each other or something?*

Trying to ignore this angst, I entered the discussion panel about international adoption, a topic of particular interest to me since I was adopted from Korea. I arrived too early, however, and the silence was deafening. My heart pounded at what seemed to be a million beats per minute, my palms were coated with a cold, clammy sweat, and my foot refused to stop tapping. Still, I managed to take a seat, creating a buffer zone for myself (sitting just close enough to see clearly, but just far enough not to be noticed).

As more and more people started to fill the empty seats, the storm of my nervousness passed, and I was able to finally sit still. The discussion began with people talking about their experiences with racism and the hostility they faced because of the way they looked. People talked about feeling like they would never ever fit in, that Asian adoptees would forever be phenotypically different and that, even though they looked the part, they would never be able to relate to their ancestral struggles. "Well, shit," I whispered to myself. This had never occurred to me. It seemed so obvious now, but somehow I had chosen to overlook this for my whole life. After hearing all of this, however, I no longer felt like an alien in a foreign land. I didn't have to decide between being white and being Asian. I was both, at the same time, among people who felt exactly the way I did.

I was home.

The subject of childhood came up. In place of memory, a void of nothingness. I couldn't seem to produce any positive, concrete recollections of my social life from pre-school until fourth grade. I went numb as I put forth every ounce of my physical and mental energy into trying to conjure at least one happy memory. I must've looked like I was overtaken by some kind of hallucinogenic drug, for I completely withdrew myself from the conference, tuning out everything but my own thoughts: *What in the hell happened to me as a kid? Was I happy? Sad? Funny? Shy? Who was I?*

Growing up in a 96%-white, middle-class suburban town in Michigan, I was never exposed to another Korean-American for most of my formative years. In fact, I was one of one-and-a-half Asians in my graduating class of 420 students. This lack of diversity inadvertently bred ignorance toward most other races and ethnicities.

When I was younger, I was always conscious of the fact that I was adopted, but the childish naivety I possessed prevented me from fully comprehending what that truly meant. I remember in third grade we were discussing the origins of our families by using our last names. I raised my hand with the confidence of an Olympic-gold medalist and proudly claimed that I was German. My classmates filled the room with quiet giggles. "You're so funny, Erica!" someone exclaimed. I didn't get it, but was so confused by their reaction that I didn't question it.

It seemed as though there was not a day that went by when I wasn't asked a question like, "Are you Chinese?" "Speak any Chinese?" "Do you remember what Korea was like?" The repetitiveness of these questions filled me with an annoyance worse than the sound of an unseen mosquito that buzzes continuously around your ear. I would become so irritated that I would sarcastically lash out with comments like, "Yep, even though I'm not even Chinese, I can totally speak it just for you!" The constant reminder that I didn't belong caused me to become full of unnecessary anger and resentment.

Because everything was such a big blur to me, I called home to ask my adoptive mother what kind of child I was. In a low, soft tone, as if she had been hiding something from me, she said, "You'd come home from school crying nearly every day. The kids would harass you by pulling their eyes back and calling you names, but you would never let me get involved out of fear of getting picked on even more. You would tell me that you hated yourself and expressed this by writing it all over the walls and furniture at home... And repeatedly, you'd tell me that I wasn't your real mom and that you were going to go back to Korea, where you thought you belonged."

Hearing this, my eyes swelled with tears of guilt, my stomach dropped to the floor, and my heart was crushed. I was speechless, but thought, *What kind of child does this to her mother? What gave me the right to say such awful things?*

Though my adoptive mom has forgiven me for speaking to her like that, I am still trying to come to terms with it. I know that we cannot control what little seven-year-olds tell each other (or what they tell their parents), but I cannot help but feel guilty for putting my adoptive mother through such pain and strife.

Due to the immense discrimination I felt from my

classmates, I didn't have any real friends until fourth grade, so I knew exactly what it felt like to have absolutely no one. I seemed to be stuck in a black hole of desolation where self-esteem was practically unheard of. Every day at recess, while my classmates were off playing and having fun, I would sequester myself away from the playground. Sitting near the door, I always yearned to go back inside, constantly thinking about how I'd never be able to escape my loneliness. One unusual day, however, a girl named Kaitlyn approached me and asked if I wanted to play. *This is too good to be true*, I thought, *After all of these years, how could someone actually see me in a positive light?* Astonished that anyone truly wanted to hang out with me, I accepted her offer and we soon became best friends. This marked the beginning of my friend-making journey and gave me a spark of hope.

It's sad for me to think about how children's identities depend so heavily on what their peers think of them. All throughout middle and high school, I allowed the people around me to dictate my actions. Since I never seemed to fit in with my classmates, I picked up the whole, "If you can't beat them, join them" mindset and started winning the approval of others by making "funny" racist jokes toward myself. The more I did it, the more people seemed to like me. I broke free from the shackles of loneliness. I was finally accepted, I finally had friends, and I was finally happy!

(But then again, "Ignorance is bliss.")

I kept this up until the last semester of my freshman year in college (after taking two Asian-American Studies classes and attending the conference). Before learning about Asian-American culture, I wrote a journal assignment in my last semester, and in it I said, "When I am asked where I am from, I tell people South Korea (because that is technically where I originated from), but then I immediately notify that person that I was adopted by a white family because I don't want people to think I'm truly Asian." Because truth and acceptance are hard things to swallow for stubborn people like me, I literally formulated the idea that I would benefit socially by ignoring my cultural identity, completely making myself believe that embracing "whiteness" would translate into more friendship.

The insatiable need to phenotypically belong controlled my every action. So much so that I even convinced myself that I hated the very taste of Chinese food. Since everyone mistook me for being Chinese, I didn't want anything to do with its culture (or any other Asian culture for that matter). Thus, the need to assimilate became a sort of drug to me. I injected the whiteness into my veins and allowed it to take over my thoughts and actions. It was an addiction that blinded me to every other aspect of my identity. If I continued to convince myself that I was a part of the dominant, mainstream, white culture, then I could convince everybody else, too (or so I thought).

In college, I realized that physical resemblance doesn't automatically allow you to fit in. Even though I wasn't okay with my Asian identity, I was looking forward to the diversity at Michigan. Maybe I would actually meet some other Asians that I could relate to, considering the lack of exposure in my hometown. During a discussion about our family histories in an introductory Asian-American Studies class, my professor, as well as many of my fellow students, told their stories. Yet again, I had nothing to articulate at the time (my adoptive family's ancestors didn't face racial discrimination, nor were my adoptive parents or grandparents first-generation immigrants). The class only had about twenty students and, of course, not all of the Asian-American students faced discrimination, but the majority of them did. As they discussed their familial struggles, I tried hard not to choke on the undeniable truth of my existence. *Who was I kidding?* I'd never be a "true" Asian. Instead, I'd just look like one. I could no longer choose to overlook who I was.

In the process of forcing myself to explore my social standings, I became aware of the fact that entirely denying one of my identities had caused me to repress it even more. Understanding that my fear of rejection stemmed from the discontent of my explicit Asian-American identity had also made me see why I was so afraid to show any other facets of my identity, particularly my sexuality. I always knew there wasn't something quite "ordinary" about how I felt, but would try to ignore it, pushing it into the back of my mind. Even though it may be quite obvious from the way I act, compared to my perfect Barbie-Girl best friends, most people do not question me about it. I never understood why I couldn't just "come out" and tell people that I am gay, but I ultimately recognized that it all came back to my need to belong and to assimilate into the dominant culture. I used to think, *If I can't even be fully comfortable with who I am on the outside, how could I love who I am on the inside? Who could possibly love and accept me if I couldn't even do this for myself?*

I've finally realized, however, that I need to transform myself, to break free from my own thoughts, to re-nature who I am, in an effort to liberate myself from my fears and to start anew. Considering that identity and personality are two of the most dynamic things that humans possess, I know that it will not be an easy task (by any means), but I know that this is something I must do. I want to change. I need to change.

My classes, and the conference, showed me a reality that woke me from a 17 and-a-half year coma of ignorance. It took many years of self-discovery, but I now recognize the honest realities of who I am, and because of this, I don't think I've ever felt this emotionally alive in my entire life. I don't know who I am yet, and maybe I will never know, but at least for now, I understand why I act the way I do today. No longer am I so full of hate (for myself or others), nor do I blame anyone for my issues, either. I am actually more than thankful for everyone who is currently in my life and try my best to prevent others from feeling any of that same kind of depression or isolation. Perhaps both my outward, and inward, identity crises were actually blessings in disguise that allowed me to love and to empathize with others more than I ever had before.

I often question why I am the way I am, but I need to stop asking why and start asking, *Why not?* There has to be a reason for my existence, but even if there isn't, then why shouldn't I just give it one? I'm not saying that I'm one-hundred-percent okay with who I am yet, but one day, hopefully, I will be.

In order to continue making progress, in both thought and action, I know that I need to start getting involved and being more proactive. Now that I am finally conscious of my social status in this world, I want to also be a catalyst for others to discover theirs, as well. To start, I am going to volunteer for a grassroots organization that allows college students to mentor 9-to-13 year-old Asian-American adoptees, enabling them to become more comfortable with themselves. I even plan to attend annual Korean adoptee conferences in the summers with my adoptive mom and adopted brother so that, as a family, we can hopefully become closer and, collectively, reach some life-changing conclusions about ourselves and about each other. I have also just recently written an oral history of a Korean-American adoptee's life and been accepted into the honors program in sociology where I will write a thesis on "The Social Construction of Race through Transracial Adoption." And, as for my sexual identity, I am looking to join a support group for LGBTQ people of color. It is both terrifying and exciting to think about these plans, but I know that I need to follow through with them because I must keep moving forward.

This is only the beginning.

Erica Gehringer is a senior undergraduate student at The University of Michigan majoring in Sociology and minoring in Asian/Pacific Islander American Studies. She was adopted from Seoul, South Korea, at the age of four-months and grew up in Commerce Township, Michigan. Within the adoption community, she is conducting research about the experiences of Korean-American adoptees and their understandings of the institution of Korean-American adoption. Additionally, as an extracurricular activity, she has started an on-campus organization called, "Girls in Friendship Together (GIFT)," that pairs young Asian-American adoptees with Asian-American adult mentors. This grassroots initiative offers an opportunity for her to reach out to and, most importantly, to learn from a community that she never knew existed before college. Ultimately, she plans to attend graduate school and then hopes to pursue a career in adoption research and social work.

Simply an American Now

I WAS BORN IN București, the capital of Romania, in October of 1986. My parents had been married for almost 25 years and had nine children together. I am the eighth child (and their last daughter). My mother was 38, and my father 46, when I came into the world. In 1990, my parents divorced and my mother had her last child. Five of my mother's 10 children were adopted internationally.

Late in December of 1989, Ceaușescu (Romania's communist leader) was ousted during a *coup d'état*. The Ceaușescus had ruled Romania for approximately four decades. Ceaușescu wanted to create a larger army and banned contraception and birth control. Couples were taxed heavily unless they had at least five children (after which they would be rewarded). Ceaușescu's secret police enforced these policies. Ceaușescu successfully increased the population, but many families could not care for their children. Food was rationed, while water, heat, and electricity were on strict schedules. In desperation, many families took their children to orphanages, usually during cold winter months.

After the fall of Ceauşescu, John Upton produced a special report about the state of Romanian orphanages for *20/20*. My adoptive parents watched this. People were horrified at what they saw on television and many of them travelled to Romania, causing a spike in demand for children. It is estimated that 30,000 children were adopted from Romania, with 10,000 taking place between 1990 and 1991 alone (the highest rate reported for any country). When families returned to the orphanages for their children, many learned that they were simply not there. The children had been adopted overseas (many without their parents' consent) and papers were forged. Others were told that their children had been moved to another (unspecified) facility. This makes me question how many adoptees are actually legal citizens of their adopted countries. False papers and sealed adoption records make it doubly difficult to trace one's origins; difficult, but not impossible.

My adoptive parents unsuccessfully tried to adopt from Ethiopia. After watching the *20/20* report, they decided to adopt from Romania and were approved for two children. By 1991 (the year that I was adopted), many foreigners were travelling to Romania in search of an "abandoned or orphaned" child. My adoptive mother joined a group of prospective couples and was paired with a travelling partner. The two of them were in Romania for approximately five weeks. On their first day, they met a priest who told them about my family's situation (things at home were temporarily unstable due to my father's retirement and my parents' divorce). Even though we were considered poor, other families were even worse off. It pains me to think that had my family, and dozens of others, been supported financially, then the drastic "solution" of overseas adoption would never have entered into the equation.

My adoptive mother and the other woman visited various orphanages, but they considered many of the children "too sick." Adopting a child from any of the orphanages looked bleak for these two women because most of the children didn't have their birth certificates with them (because their families hadn't planned for them to be adopted). A birth certificate, along with the mother's consent, was the minimum requirement needed to adopt a child. Many foreigners learned that it was easier to go to the countryside, or directly to the mother's home, in order to harass and/or bribe them until they finally "agreed" to relinquish their children. When coercion or manipulation are factors, free will is extinguished. This, I was told as an adult, violates the intent of the United Nations Convention on the Rights of the Child, which states that children have a right to their identity in their home countries, and a right to be raised by their families. Poverty is simply not an adequate reason for a child to be adopted out of a country.

My adoptive mother wanted to adopt me as soon as she saw me and it was easier for her to follow through on this idea because I wasn't in an orphanage. After she spoke with my mother, it was "agreed" that I would be adopted with my 11-year-old sister. My other sister, who was six, was adopted by the other woman. On a layover back to the States, my adoptive mother and the other woman met an unmarried Canadian woman headed for Romania. They told her about my family and she adopted my eight-year-old sister just weeks later.

The sister I was adopted with wrote to our family often. My brother missed me and our sister and wanted to come to America. In 1993, when he was 15, he was placed into the same adoptive family with us. In 1995, we were introduced to another 15-year-old Russian "orphan" who was also placed into the household. My adoptive father was 45 and his wife was 26 at the time of my adoption. They had two sons together, and he also had two daughters from a previous marriage.

We moved a lot. In 1999 (when I was 12), a neighbor told me that my Romanian father had died in a car accident. His letters never came again. Shortly after this, my adoptive parents divorced and I was bounced around from house-to-house, literally unwanted. In 2001, when I was 15, my brother committed suicide at age 23. My adoptive mother kicked me out shortly thereafter. I moved to Washington State to live with my adoptive father and his new Russian wife. In my senior year of high school, my adoptive father sold the house and moved away. I was left to fend for myself.

After I lost a job in my early 20s, I decided to look into my own background. I researched adoption practices and history, joined adoption groups on Facebook, and even opened a group for Romanian adoptees. *To Romania, With Love: Saving the World One Child at a Time*, by Mary Albanese, hints at the coercion and bribery that were used to persuade my family to "let me and my siblings go." My life changed drastically when I read *Romania: For Export Only: The Untold Story of the Romanian 'Orphans,'* by Roelie Post, a European Commission civil servant who documented unethical adoption practices. I realized that I am living proof of child trafficking under the guise of adoption. Oftentimes, what is portrayed as a selfless act is far from the reality of the corrupt practice. Many adoptive parents pass home inspections, but there are rarely any follow-ups.

Romania has extensively altered its child welfare system. Many orphanages have been replaced by foster care and more residential homes. Romania became a member of the European Union in 2007 and has been working extremely hard to meet all EU standards, which includes designating international adoption as the last resort for a child in crisis. Even though Romania is actively trying to cultivate a positive image, many people still view it exactly as it was perceived in the early 90s. If more people realized how much the country has actually changed, it could become even greater.

People tend to assume that I was adopted by people who "loved" me, but adoption does not always equal love. In fact, love often has little to do with strangers incorporating foreign children into their "forever families." Their "love" for me paled in comparison to their affection for their own children. Because of this, I've never thought of myself as "blessed." It is not "special" to have been "chosen [or] rescued." Adoption forcibly removed me from my homeland and the arms of my father. *Where is the beauty in losing my entire family in a single day and* forever being labeled an "orphan" (even though I had living parents)? Where is the blessing in pretending that another family is my own? What is so special about being forced to perpetuate this lie for the rest of my life?

I have lived many lives, most of them in poverty. I was treated differently growing up because I was "rescued" and I was supposed to forget my past and be "grateful" because I was "simply an American now." I have memories of Romania, but was never allowed to talk about them unless it was to reporters who were writing the latest article about Westerners rescuing Romanian orphans.

I started college in July of 2013 and decided to return to Romania in October that same year. I wasn't able to find all the answers that I sought, but I haven't stopped trying, either. Every step I take in the United States is one more step away from my true identity. It has been difficult to be a foreigner here. Everything that happened to me was somehow expected to be okay, but it wasn't (and it isn't). I may have been raised in the United States, but my heart has always been with my family in Romania. I eventually came to realize that adoption is not a guarantee of a "better" life, but it does guarantee a "different" life. The material objects I have received in the United States could have easily been obtained in Romania without having to lose my heritage, language, customs, or time with my family. The search for myself seems never ending.

Georgiana-A. Macavei lives in Washington State, holds an associate's degree in pre-law from Olympic College, and has plans to attend law school. She enjoys reading, creating art, and is currently writing a memoir. She is also in the process of relearning Romanian and plans to return to her homeland permanently. Updates on her activism can be found on Facebook at "Romanian Adoptees Worldwide – RAW."

Magnitude 7.3

I WAS BORN IN Haiti in 1979 and adopted in 1984 by a single French woman. The story of my abandonment boiled down to a few vague lines and other falsehoods written in my adoption file. It wasn't until 2002 that I managed to find my Haitian family and only then did I learned the truth about my adoption.

There are three entities in me:

- Manassé, the Haitian child who arrived in France in 1984
- Christophe, the perfect little French boy who started to exist in 1984
- Tinan, who appeared in 2004

It is not easy for three people to inhabit the same body.

Excerpt 1

My Haitian mother, Iliasia, could not have children (despite numerous attempts) and her sterility made her very unhappy. One day, Iliasia's husband proposed that he leave Haiti for the United States (prompted by his growing prosperity) and Iliasia accepted the idea. After they sold all of their possessions, her husband actually left for the United States leaving Illiasia homeless, penniless, and alone with her infertility. After several years of misery, Iliasia met another Haitian man and their union produced a daughter who died five days after birth. Iliasia despaired after the infant's death. But one day, my older brother was born, a frail child who was often ill when he was young. He survived but, at the same time, our parent's relationship began to deteriorate.

Things got worse after the arrival of their second child. My mother, 38-years-old at the time of my birth, baptized me as Manassé. Like my brother, I was also fragile and needed care. During my early childhood, Iliasia found herself, once again, without a partner and without work. This time, however, she carried two young children in her arms. Our survival became precarious. In Haiti at the time, it was customary to entrust children, for short periods of time, in a type of boarding school run by a religious congregation that received foreign aid. Children placed in their care temporarily always belonged to their Haitian parents. The nursery was built to give children in need some help such as food, medicine, and education. My big brother was placed in a facility of this type not far from our hometown, but he failed to adapt. Iliasia brought him packages, but the gifts were turned away, and the children remained poor as a result.

Iliasia retrieved my older brother, who was then in very poor health, even though she was still unable to provide for her two sons. She decided to put me in the home of Miss Marthe in Gros Morne, seventy-five miles away, which was a nursery of about forty children. It operated on a principle of exchange with France. A man, named Wisly, placed Haitian children with

French host families so that they could get treatment and receive an education. He then brought them back to Haiti in either a few months or a few years.

It was expected that a permanent relationship would be maintained between the adoptive French family and the Haitian one, except that the children who were adopted to France never returned to Haiti! Haitian parents had very little information about their children, or about their French guardians, and contact was cut off after only a few months. Wisly, who was supposed to serve as a bridge between the two countries and the two families, vanished. Rumors also circulated that children had died or had been used for organ trafficking. From all of those who went missing at the time, only the two oldest children from the nursery managed to return to Haiti as adults to find their families. I was the third to take advantage of this opportunity but, among the three children who returned, no one has been able to find information about the other missing children.

I met with Haitian mothers of adoption loss, the victims of child trafficking still left behind. They shared both their pain, but also their hope, with me. I promised to look for their roughly forty missing sons and daughters once I was back in France. This recovery mission has become my *raison d'être*.

Between 2002 and 2003, I returned to Haiti. I took up the responsibility of financing the education of my newly-discovered little brother and sister. I felt compelled to take on the burden for my family and for all to go well yet, despite our regular exchanges, I felt more and more foreign and alienated from my homeland.

Excerpt 2

In 2002, I believed that I was at a crossroads in my life, but I am now starting to realize that that was not the case. In 2003, I felt great doubt. On my first trip to Haiti, I thought that I belonged to two worlds. It occurs to me now that I do not belong to either. When I left France, I needed to find my roots because I did not feel at home there. But, as the years go by, I realize I am no more at home in Haiti. I have friends and a lot of people who appreciate and support me but, yet, I feel alone and out of context. I wander in a no-man's land, ill-defined, trying to build upon my shaky foundation, while it continually gives way under my feet. Sometimes, I struggle to keep my balance and not to get lost in the grey area of adoption. Sometimes, I lose my grip completely and falter. I do not have vertigo, but every time I stumble, my heart drops, and I feel worse. I sometimes struggle with madness. To keep my feet firmly planted on the ground, I have to focus my effort on concrete and logical things to keep sane. In high school, and at the beginning of my graduate studies, I was not very good in math (despite my appetite for science). I improved significantly, however, as my need for roots intensified, I would seek concrete, immutable certainties, as well as rigor and logic in order to stay grounded.

My adoptive mother does not understand me. Our relationship is riddled with disputes and conflict. I have no adoptive father, someone to balance her authority. I also feel that my girlfriend does not fully understand me, which has caused issues between us, as she moves so easily in the world as she pursues her dreams. Despite my best efforts, I cannot get closer to her. My Haitian family does not understand me, either. My older Haitian brother is the only one with whom I have a healthy and peaceful relationship with, but we communicate infrequently via e-mail and sometimes on the phone. I don't blame anyone. There is no need to do math to realize that I am the common denominator in all of these relationships.

In 2004, tensions with my Haitian family were high and conflicts with my adopter were so destructive that I decided to finally cut ties with my French family in order to survive.

Excerpt 3

Locked in an icy cocoon, my older brother sends me e-mail that I do not read because I'm barricaded in my solitude. My fiancée no longer talks to me. I'm gone. It is the last heartbeat of Christophe (my French name). Someone (or some thing) else is still present, but the little French boy who was much loved by his adoptive mother, has died.

Failing to mourn for myself, I try to remove all traces of who I was. I separate from my girlfriend, I move, change my phone number, and register with the *liste rouge*. I left without warning anyone – not even my friends. I leave fake addresses so that my adoptive mother cannot find me. I threw out all objects that remind me of my past life.

I am no longer Christophe. To continue to exist, I become Tinan. More than a name, it is a concept, a means of survival, an identity that I have to build piece-by-piece. I untangle who I was supposed to be, to erase my reflexes, my ingrained habits. I reset my brain like a hard drive to be wired before installing a new operating system. Thus, I continue to live my own way. I do my best to move forward, despite the obstacles. I help others whenever I am able, those who firmly believe that life is beautiful. I fulfill my duties, I try to accomplish my mission, to provide as much happiness as possible. It's all that I can do to keep from giving up.

I model Tinan like a cyborg. My body is what it is, but my brain can do whatever it wants. To get rid of anything that resembles a genetic disorder, I choose to become impervious to certain sensations like pain, hunger, thirst, fatigue, stress, cold, or anxiety. I used to get sick very often, but I won't get sick anymore. I used to be very ticklish, now that is over. I decided that I will no longer feel anger and that I will never cry again. The ataraxia is not far.

What is Tinan's future? I know I cannot keep my life in a robotic state but, for now, I haven't found another solution. Gradually, my shell became a prison that I could not escape with bars forged by my sensitivity, my weakness, my fears, my shyness, my lack of confidence, and my need for love.

The years pass and I am hyperactive. I teach salsa. I create a dance company. I invent choreographies. I play the saxophone in several bands. I study music very intensely, including its composition and its history. I write and arrange different styles for multiple groups and I feel a great need to create and to make art. I know that soon I will resign from the Department of Education. As a physics teacher, I am cast in a role that is not creative enough. My days are too long and my nights are too short. My body is worn, but numb, I do not listen to its warnings. I used to take up to ten micro-naps several times a day, which allowed me to recover partly from my lack of rest. I've become efficient in the art of analysis, making syntheses, and creating models to understand how things work. These new capabilities are very helpful to me when I teach, allowing me to better understand the difficulties of my students and to better deconstruct the steps involved with reasoning or the individual components of various movements so that I can explain it in detail, make it easy to grasp, and accessible to anyone.

Excerpt 4

I am a free and lonely man, but I cannot find stability, because it would require that I accept the brute part of my being, which I refuse. I try hard to contain the demon which is imprisoned in my cell, but it is a constant struggle against myself. I'm finally starting to understand the exact nature of this monstrous creature. It is the small child within me, Manassé, whose growth and life are suddenly arrested at the age of four and-a-half, when he fell into this nightmare without end, sent far from his family, from his country, far from the love of his Haitian mother.

By dint of incarceration, secretly declining the hostile world that was offered to him as a gift, Manassé eventually became a wild beast, extremely violent, and dangerous (but with a pure soul of a fragile child). *What a paradox!* The being I consigned to oblivion in 2004 was Christophe. Yet Manassé was there for twenty years. If I want to live in peace, I have to release the prisoner. But the wrath of Manassé is so big that it will destroy everything in its path, devouring Tinan (as it did Christophe). *What will become of me if I open Manassé's cage? Will I be a monster?* My integrated personality and these twenty long years of frustration and pent-up anger will lead me to the irreparable. As a result, I cannot love myself or accept love from anybody. To calm Manassé's anger, I would have to admit that what happened to me was not my fault. I should also forgive the adults responsible, even if they are guilty.

I hold enormous grudges against my two mothers.

In 1984, Iliasia did not abandon me. She dropped me off at a boarding school for a few months in the hopes of getting me back to full health. She was deceived into signing an "abandonment for adoption" paper. Like the majority of Haitian mothers at the time, she could not read. It made no difference to Manassé whether or not Iliasia had abandoned him voluntarily the day he was forced to board a plane for nowhere without understanding what was happening. It was her responsibility to look after her son and to not be manipulated. Ignorance might have been a mitigating factor, but it was, by no means, an excuse.

My adoptive mother has always believed that I should thank her for "saving" me. *How can you thank someone for removing you from family roots? How can we pretend that money and a Parisian apartment are worth more than a Haitian mother's love? This is absurd, of course!* Adoption, itself, is an absurd idea. It should be a workaround, a last resort, the ultimate solution before euthanasia. Instead, it has become the answer to the whims and desires of Western families. They adopt for themselves because they cannot have children, because they need someone to inherit their hopes and frustrations, or because they want to brag that they've saved a little dark-skinned child from certain death. I was adopted by a French woman for these three reasons and, for these three reasons, I can never forgive her.

Before learning the truth about his adoption, **Tinan Leroy** thought (as most French people do), that it was a good thing. He even felt guilty for not being grateful to his adoptive mother. But a return to his home country of Haiti, the subsequent years spent searching, investigating, studying, and meeting a lot of other adoptees, and writing the book, *Magnitude 7.3*, led him to this horrible conclusion: Inter-country adoption is just a huge marketplace where children are sold, resold, exchanged, and trafficked without any real regard for their actual welfare. Many adoptions have dramatic endings, but these numerous cases are rarely reported. The truth is that adopted children are nothing more than luxury goods. The powerful adoption lobby prohibits any study showing this aspect of the industry, which is the reason Tinan is firmly determined to reveal the hidden face of adoption in order to seek some redress for the victims of this particular type of trafficking.

Update: On October 19, 2014, Tinan Leroy passed away from heart failure. While he was alive, Tinan asked that fellow adoptees support his story "because the French will not acknowledge the hidden side of international adoption." The love affair with the practice of adoption has become a global crisis. During Tinan's short life, he was a very talented man: an author, a physics professor, a saxophone player, and a choreographer, but he confided that he felt alone. His friends believe that his adopter deleted his Facebook, YouTube, author, and memorial pages. A lack of support from adopters is reported as a common problem for adopted people who search for their families. Our hope is to keep Tinan's memory alive through this book. Tinan wanted this book to reach the mainstream public. Please consider donating copies on his behalf to educational institutions and organizations.

Nightmares Are Dreams, Too

I WAS BORN IN India, but I do not know my actual birth date. I always felt strongly and have fleeting memories that I was well loved and cared for in the early part of my life. Around the age of three- or four-years-old while I was sleeping, a woman stole me from my bed and my family in the night. The details are too much to go into, but I am compiling the story of my early years into a book.

In 1974, I arrived at Holy Angels Convent in Thiruvananthapuram, the capital of the Indian state of Kerala. I was taken very good care of by the Catholic nuns while I lived there. The nuns called me "Latha" until I was baptized and named "Mary Magdalen." The years that I lived at the convent held happy memories for me. I was fed well, clothed, and educated. We slept on mats, and we did not have a lot of material things, but I was happy. I was a young girl, lighter skinned than the other children. They would call me "cat," but it was never in a mean way that I felt I was being bullied or anything. I was never sexually or physically abused there. One time I remember pulling myself up and looking over the wall of the convent and seeing a house next door with a wonderful swimming pool. When I saw the pool, I wanted one so bad. After that, I went into the huge shower stall and plugged the drain with a cloth and turned on both shower heads full blast so that I could go swimming. For that, I got in trouble. The nun tried not to laugh when she went to spank me. Another nun, Sister Mary, had a little dog which was a Pomeranian named Bruni. Bruni was my constant shadow, slept with me every night, and was a constant comfort for me.

One day a man came to take individual photos of a few of us children who were at the orphanage, and I was one of them. A picture that was taken of me had a write up which said, "Latha likes reading so much that she picks up whatever paper or book she finds. She is clever at studies. She is fond of singing and dancing. On the whole she is a bright child and good at sports." I was then informed a few months later that I was going to be adopted to a wonderful loving family in Canada. Then the preparations started. There were five of us girls being adopted at the same time. After we were taken to Madras by train and sent before a judge for the adoption to be legalized, we returned to the convent to wait.

Then the day came for four of us to be sent to Canada. Sister Mary then took us by plane to Madras where we stayed one night in a convent there. The next morning we were taken to the airport. Before Sister Mary said goodbye to us, she pulled me aside and told me that all my dreams were going to come true in Canada. Little did I know then that nightmares are dreams, too. We were then put into the care of a woman with a baby on the flight. This woman accompanied us all the way to Toronto, Ontario, where she had reached her destination to deliver the baby to a couple there. We were then put under the care of the stewardesses for the remainder of the trip to Calgary, Alberta.

It was night when we arrived and we were met there by the families who had adopted us. I was adopted along with another girl to the same family. We stayed one night in a hotel. We were so excited we kept looking at all the lights outside. I was beaten by my adoptive mother for that and was told in a mean manner to go to bed.

That was my first experience with the new adoptive parents. The next morning we were taken to McDonald's and fed an egg McMuffin for breakfast. My body was not used to Western fast food, and I began to vomit while eating. My new adoptive mother started shoving the sandwich down my throat telling me I could be starving in India.

We then left for their house in British Columbia. The adoptive couple lived just outside of a small city, called Nelson. I was given the birthdate of May 18, 1969, even though I have no idea what my real birthdate is. (*So many people take this for granted!*) Mr. and Mrs. Pearce then changed my name to "Vanessa."

I quickly learned and experienced that Mrs. Pearce was a cold and abusive woman who should not have been allowed to have children (let alone animals). I was literally kept in the attic of their home. The attic was freezing cold in the winter and stifling hot in the summer. I could barely even stand up in the room. There was a single bed in there, and nothing else – and I mean nothing. Not even a light. I was not allowed in the living room except to clean like a maid. Not allowed to watch television, touch the fridge or stove. I was not allowed to get out of bed until I was told I could. Everything was very controlled in the household by Mrs. Pearce. All I can say is that prisoners lived better than me. I was always scared and jumpy because I never knew when I would get a beating for no reason.

In the early months even though Mrs. Pearce was cruel, her husband would give me books and food when she would deny me food for periods of time. The books helped me escape, even temporarily, from my living hell. By being kind to me, Mr. Pearce earned my trust. Then all of a sudden one day while I was allowed to play the piano, he came up behind me and grabbed me and he had an erection and started humping against me. This is when the sexual abuse began. I had no safe place to turn. Sleep became my only friend because it was the only time I could escape and forget the horror I was going through.

School was not much better. The surrounding communities were predominantly white. I was bullied by children for being of a different colour. I really started to believe that there was something wrong with me and that I was truly unlovable. This especially rang true when Christmas came. All I heard from the other kids was about Santa Claus and how he loved all children. Yet, on Christmas Day, all I found was a note in my stocking saying that I was a bad girl and if I was a better girl the next year he might bring me something. So, I thought even Santa Claus hated me. I felt I had no place to be safe except when I fell asleep.

I always felt cold and hungry and I missed India – the convent, the nuns, the warm weather, and being treated kindly. I was finally able to get a letter off to Sister Mary begging her to take me back to India. She replied that she could not bring me back and to say my *Hail Mary's*. After receiving this from the one person whom I still trusted and thought could keep me safe, I lost all hope. After being beaten again for unknown reasons, I found a can of turpentine and drank it and began to vomit. My adoptive mother dragged me by my hair into the attic and left me there to die. My adoptive parents left abruptly in their car. By some miracle, I have survived.

Because my adoptive family had money and were deemed important in the community, they were allowed to adopt me. I felt so alone and felt like an outsider (as I was a woman of colour in a predominantly white community). This is the wonderful Western country where Sister Mary told me all my dreams would come true. But, nightmares are dreams, too.

Vanessa Pearce is 44-years-old and lives in Canada. Since 2006, she has worked actively and passionately in the areas of human rights and adoption reform. She wants to end the myth that adoption always leads to a better life. "It has to be recognized that, like Aboriginal children who were taken away from their parents and forced into residential school, abused international adoptees have also been taken from their countries, lost their culture, and faced sexual, physical, and mental abuse, as well." Vanessa is now working on a memoir and seeking justice for her two sons (particularly for her older son, Matthew, who died tragically in 2012). Going public with her story is just the beginning of the promise that she made to him.

In Memory of Appa

AFTER SEALING MY DESTINY back in 1970, I wonder how that adoption worker could sleep at night. He finished his task and went home that day, exhausted from all of his good deeds. *How could he play God?* When he wrote down lies in my file, I'm sure that he followed rules. The agency employee must have had guidelines about what to write in order to make the documents seem true enough, to make the process more efficient. They had to maintain a certain number of kids to be adopted at all times (and, of course, it was better to have as many as possible). As the South Korean orphanage earned more for overseas adoptions than for domestic ones, there was a built-in incentive to send kids abroad.

I wonder if the staff feels the weight of their conscience when they know that they have falsified so many documents for so many children worldwide. I've wondered many times whether it might have been the same social worker that received me in 1969, who sat in the office when my father returned to bring me home again, one day in the early seventies. The staff member must have looked my *appa* square in the eyes and told him the biggest lie ever—that my father would have to go and look for me at another orphanage, even though the employee knew very well that I had been sent abroad. So my father began to search for me at orphanage, after orphanage, after orphanage, all over South Korea, a search which lasted for several years, until he died in sorrow and despair.

When my *appa* handed me over to the orphanage, he wasn't told that he would never see me again. (If they had, he most certainly would never have let them take me.) *Why did they lie to him about where I was? Was it because they wanted money for the information (and he didn't have enough to pay what they demanded)?* I've been told that this was a common practice at many orphanages in those days.

So here I am today, an angry, sad adoptee, wanting to tell the world that a huge injustice has been done to me and to my Korean father (who was desperate to get help for his children in need). This has also affected my oldest sister's life, because she, too, searched for me for many years. She was only a teenager when she started after she promised our *appa*, on his deathbed, that she would continue his search so that we could be together. She yearned for me for so many years. She is my hero. Only after our reunion in 1986 has she had peace in her heart.

Our father loved all of his children, but he needed help during a difficult time to make a better life for us. It was sixteen years after The Korean War ended, and after our mother died suddenly, so help was greatly needed. My story is not unique, but rather a typical sad event that exemplifies this sentence perfectly: *Adoption is a permanent solution to a temporary problem.* It hurts so many and affects so many aspects of our lives. Today, I have very little contact with my sisters because of difficulties with language, differences in culture, and the fact that, although we are family, we are also strangers.

Adoption adversely affects everything in our lives. We lose our parents (most importantly our mothers) which leaves deep emotional scars (otherwise known as the "the primal wound"). But we also lose the life we were meant to have, our heritage, and so much more. All I can do now is pick up little pieces here and there in an attempt to reconstruct my story.

Many of us, who were adopted at a young age and are now adults, are looking into our pasts, digging up our origins, and uncovering the old sins of the adoption system. Hopefully, the world will see us and begin to understand that the adoption industry is cruel and unloving and, that by adopting children, adoptive parents are supporting that industry. Today, many are working to end the adoption business in order to raise awareness about the fates of children sent overseas. This is my only comfort when I think back at my time in Korea prior to being removed and my abusive childhood in Norway. I hope the grief has not all been for nothing.

I feel if my *appa* knew I was trying to change the world in this little way (to make it so no more children will have to experience the ocean of tears and grief), he would be proud of me.

My Dear *Appa*:

Rest in Peace. You died in July of 1974 (when I was 5 years old in Norway). If I had only known then that you had come back to take me home! I wonder if you would have recognized me. Would you have seen the sorrow in my eyes, would you have eased my pain, and would you have loved me as much as you did my other sisters? In my heart, I know the answer and will always treasure you.

Your Khara

A Father's Legacy to his Daughter

How to unravel my past and cope with my losses and sadness?

Once, many years ago, I had hopes of reuniting with my *appa*. I was in South Korea, my Korean family had been found, and I was face-to-face with my real sisters. My father, they told me, had died twelve years ago. In that one swift moment my hope turned to dust and, despite the indescribable joy of meeting my family for the first time, the bottom fell out of my soul and I felt empty and unbelievably lonely. Even today, I have no words to describe it. I'm almost ashamed to admit that, despite everything, I was terribly disappointed and saddened that my father wasn't there. I had travelled so far, not knowing whether I would find anyone, but still hoping with every fibre of my body that he would be there. That I would return as a daughter who had weathered a rough childhood in a land far, far away and only wanted to come home for a moment, to turn back the clock and feel his embrace and love. I had been saving up for that moment for years.

Instead, I was devastated that I had lost him again and, this time, lost him forever. Even today, more than twenty-five years later, the tears come welling up whenever I think about our separation.

I look out the window and see rain pouring down, as if the heavens know my grief and weep with me. When the skies are angry and the thunder roars, they're shouting for justice at my side. And when the rainbow stands there, colourful and bright, it reminds me of the peace and forgiveness that I seek. I do not know where to find that which my soul seeks. No bandage or plaster cast can repair the wounds (neither glue nor staples can stitch them back together). No one can bring the precious gift of peace of mind. Only one man could do that and he is forever lost. There is nothing left, no memories, no keepsakes, or souvenirs. Just a faded old photo remains to show me his face, a shadow from another time.

My sisters told me that you were thinking of me until the day you died. You never forgot, you came back for me, and you never meant for me to be gone. And right before you died, you said that I had to be reunited with my sisters.

Tears are running down my face. When I close my eyes, I see the shadow of a young man in a desperate search for his daughter from one childrens' home after another. (How I wish that I had been there for you to find!)

You were there when I came into the world. You were there for our umma, *you who delivered me when I was born, and you who gave me my name. You looked at the stars when you named me, and that is what my name means, "A Shining Star." It's as if I can hear you say, "Do you not see how they shine for you, up there in the sky? Look, that's your own little star up there!"*

For many years, I had to suppress his precious gift (my name) since it did not please people in the West. Now, forty years later, I have taken it back, though I must admit that I did not see until now what a gift it really was. It was denied to me while I was growing up (as my adoptive parents didn't like it at all and wanted to wipe out my past). It simply did not exist in their eyes. But now that they are both gone, I am finally free to reclaim what my father gave me so many years ago.

This is all that I have left of you. My uncle (your brother) told me how you chose my name with my mother (the love of your life) and that you picked a modern one for me (one that you liked very much). She was your universe, and your children were your little stars (all six of us), like the tail of a comet. Two were lost long before I was born and I hope that you have all found each other again in the heavenly realms.

In my heart, I send up eight rice lanterns into the air. One for you and one for mother, one for my brother and one for my sister who died so young, and four more for each sister who remains here. May that family of lanterns ride far on the winds in your honour and burn long and bright to signify that, in time, we will be together as a family again, forever.

At the age of one year, **Khara** was adopted from South Korea by a Caucasian family in Norway. Now in her forties, she blogs to help heal from traumas (from both the adoption and an abusive childhood with her adoptive parents) and to enlighten the world about the dark side of adoption. She says, "I wish to be a part of the machinery that will turn the world around from its view of adoption as something beautiful [to] reveal the lies for what they really are. My dream is for adoption to end."

Adoptee

Standing at a distance,
They do not know we watch.
They move with consistence,
The same genetic swatch.

The bones match each others'
Their mannerisms alike.
The face of the mother,
Plastered on little tyke.

Brother runs like father,
Apple of daddy's eye.
Genetics, no bother
Blood money cannot buy.

Sold into blindness,
Millions throughout the world,
Living without likeness,
Their pasts having been hurled.

They're told to be "thankful,"
Told their loss was for love.
They're forced to be grateful,
No savior from above.

Standing at a distance,
The world ignores our gaze.
We are the forgotten,
Alone, for all our days.

"The name I have long chosen for myself is **Cryptic Omega**, which means 'Unknown End.' For, if you do not know your history and your beginnings, how can you truly know your journey? And, if you do not know your path, how can you know your end?"

PART 2: *Unknown*

Letter from a Grounded New Yorker

Dear Mr. Governor and Deputy Secretary Saunders,

My purpose in writing your offices today is to request your support of Bills A8410/S5269 known as "The Adoptee Bill of Rights." This legislation will grant equal rights to adult adoptees born in New York State by providing us access to our "original" birth certificates.

Original birth certificates differ greatly from the "Certificate of Live Birth" New York State currently issues adoptees. While the original birth certificate contains our factual identifying information, the "amended" certificate is erroneously written as though our adoptive families are our parents. This practice in today's society continues to misguide the general public (as well as policy makers). Even President Barack Obama has faced scrutiny of late for having an amended "birth" certificate similar to those issued to adoptees in New York State.

Due to these outdated practices, adoptees in New York State are not receiving the same rights non-adoptees have as U.S. citizens. In 2004, the 9-11 Commission created "The Western Hemisphere Travel Initiative" demanding stricter practices with the granting of a U.S. passport for travel. Nationwide, adult American-born adoptees have randomly encountered rejection in their applications for a U.S. passport. The information contained on our sealed birth certificate has birth information necessary to fulfill Federal passport requirements while the amended "birth" certificates do not.

Currently, the State Department not only demands extensive detailed proof of birth information, it also demands a non-refundable application fee. Many adult adoptees wait weeks, if not months, for a passport only to have it returned marked "Action Not Taken" while also forfeiting their $100 payment.

This denial of our constitutional rights is unfair as we are American-born residents who are treated like second-class citizens. As a late-discovery adoptee, I am included in the group of adoptees who are denied in their passport application. Ironically, it was a result of the federal passport requirement that I learned of my adoption (at the age of 41) in 2007.

There are over 6 million adult adoptees living in the United States today. It is time for New York State to join Maine, Oregon, Kansas, Alaska, Alabama, and New Hampshire by granting adult adoptees, like myself, with equal access to our actual birth certificates. Won't you please join us by supporting passage of "The Adoptee Bill of Rights?"

Sincerely Yours,

Jeffrey A. Hancock
Western New York Regional Coordinator
New York Statewide Adoption Reform's Unsealed Initiative

[Note: This letter was presented to Ms. Wendy Saunders at the State Capitol on September 2, 2009.]

Being a late-discovery adoptee (as of 2007) has been a life-changing experience for **Jeff Hancock**. "Life, as you have always known it to be as fact, becomes a lifetime filled with lies in under a moment… Life, as you have always known it to be, ceases and you struggle to find your niche." The niche Jeff found centers around The Adoptee Rights Coalition. Jeff began to write articles and to be interviewed on television and radio on the topics of sealed records and equal access to original birth certificates. In 2009, Jeff attended his first adoptee rights demonstration and realized that he had found his tribe. In 2013, Jeff became ARC President. Today he works as a college tutor and freelance artist in Rochester, New York. With the support of his wife and two sons, Jeff's mission is to educate the public on the need for equal access to original birth certificates.

Without a Trace

State Secret

AFTER MY 1958 ADOPTION HEARING in a Wisconsin courtroom, I was legally re-named "Tracy Ann" and handed over to Sev and Edie DeMeyer. An orphan they named "Joey" arrived in 1958. Trained as foster parents, Edie and Sev, my adoptive mom and replacement dad, had tried to have their own babies, but couldn't. Adopting me meant they'd have their family, first me then, hopefully, a boy. Amid the "oohs" and "ahhs" of this joyous occasion, had my new family considered my heredity or the parent cells of my DNA that had actually created my body? Had anyone considered what it was like to be thrust into a sea of new faces?

No. Instead, they celebrated. They had no idea that I was devastated by the loss of my own mother. They knew they had a big job ahead of them, raising me and "Joseph William." They assumed we'd be okay. No one thought otherwise. They didn't know, or even seem to care, who I really was. My Native American blood was, somehow, a secret. We just did not talk about it. Obviously, I'd adapt and their identity would become my own.

Infertility

My adoptive mom never told me about the two babies she lost. For her, infertility must have been heartbreaking, a pain I can't fully imagine. I heard about her miscarriages from "Joey's" wife, Tracy Lea. When "Joey" married her in 1980, I became "Trace" and have used this name ever since.

Tracy Lea heard how doctors did a total hysterectomy when my adoptive mom was just 28. She probably had endometriosis, which is operable. Curable, even. That had to be hard on her and probably why she never mentioned her miscarriages to me.

The 1950s were primetime for the adoption experiment. My adoptive father was 31 and my adoptive mother was 35 when I was born in 1956. She converted to his Catholic religion before they married in 1948. I don't think it was her idea to adopt. It's just what infertile couples did in those days.

Before I arrived in 1957, my adoptive parents were foster parents to a little girl, named Cathy. "We were going to keep her, but Catholic Charities took her away. She was not adoptable, or legally free, like you," I was told. There are moments when I do remember Cathy. I even named a doll after her. I just can't remember her face. *If my adoptive parents loved her, where are Cathy's baby photos?* I could never find any. There is no trace of her. There are no newborn baby pictures of me, either. *Why did it take so long for me to be adopted?* I may never know.

Sickly

When I arrived in 1957, I'd scream when my adoptive mom tried to lay me on my stomach. I didn't cry. The back of my head was bald. I suffered with chronic ear infections, stomach aches, constipation, skin rashes, and itchy hives well into grade school, but my adoptive mom said they loved me through it. Of course, our family doctor gave me antibiotics in those days (now considered ineffective and possibly dangerous). Over-use of antibiotics was common then and I was allergic to penicillin. Very early on, my immune system did not work very well. Now I find out that my skin was telling me I had allergies. It was hard to tell when I was sick, but my adoptive mom said she could tell by looking in my eyes. (*What was I, a zombie?*) I look sad in many photos, but apparently this was no cause for alarm. They figured I'd grow out of it.

Good "Daughter"

Over time, our little family of four grew inseparably linked. I flourished, yes. As quickly as I grew, so did the uneasiness. I knew I was different. Something wasn't right. My friend, Rhonda, remembers wanting to run away at age four. I had the feeling, too, that home wasn't really home. I wanted to be someplace else. Perhaps Edie felt this, too. My adoptive mom would say to me, "You act like you don't like me." There was a reason. She was not my mother. Children are quite honest when they are confused. I had questions. So much didn't make sense.

I hid any sign of desperation and confusion. There were no words for my uneasiness, nor could I fathom how to deal with it. While my friends were running around thinking about grades and boys, I just worried about everything. While not quite sure what my brain was telling me, I tried to act normal. (Well, at least I thought I did.)

I never had a bad experience with my extended adoptive family, really. I was treated just like the rest of my cousins. All my aunts were kind. Some paid very close attention. I'm sure they watched with curiosity, as ours was the only family with adopted kids. I got real good at hiding my thoughts (which were locked up just like my adoption records, tucked away in a courthouse vault somewhere, buried in total darkness). Sometimes it scared me. *Why was I adopted? What was wrong with me?* It had to be horrible.

Part of me stayed hidden, pretending to be a good "daughter," "sister," classmate, friend. Someone called me "bubbly" (I was that good as a kid). Luckily, I discovered I could become a new person at will. I could create a happy personality who could handle anything, do anything, and be anything. I looked fearless. Blocking the confusion from my mind was sick, but a safety net. No one knew how lousy I felt. I had no clue I was grieving. Parts of my brain didn't function until much later, not until I started to wake up to all of the buried memories.

This is the splitting sickness and it can be dangerous. Fatal, even.

Reasons

My adoptive mom gave us lots of valid reasons for them to adopt. They tried to have babies, but couldn't. They were Catholic and wanted kids. That was their reason. So we believed them. They wanted us. Our parents didn't.

By trial-and-error, "Joey" and I learned not to bring up the subject and to act grateful. We understood that our predicament had conditions: If we became a problem, we'd be out on our own, possibly abandoned again, put out on the street, sent back to the orphanage, or back to foster care. No way. We could not risk that. We could not protest the absurdity or secrecy we lived under. It was never clear how they might respond to questions. She was usually bothered by something or sick. He could get real angry. We knew showing too much interest in our adoption was definitely risky. If we asked too many questions, they'd think us ungrateful.

I wonder how many kids out there acted like I did? I was confused and very sad. Some kids possibly overreact, or won't pretend, and act badly.

When I got cold, I told myself, *Remember they gave you a home. Only ask questions at the right time, whenever the subject comes up. Don't act overly interested, just curious.* It seemed necessary to disguise my need for an identity early on. My adoptive parents had absolutely no idea how I really felt or what this charade was doing to me or "Joey." I remember thinking, *My family is out there. I was taken from them. I never said it was okay with me. They might miss me.*

The threat of being abandoned again hurt so much that I silenced my curiosity and I grieved in stages. My adoptive mother often said I was moody.

"You're Only as Sick as Your Secrets"

No one had ever called me an orphan to my face. That is until Archie, my adoptive uncle Chet's brother showed up for "Joey's" high school graduation, and told me how "Joey" and I turned out okay, considering how we were both orphans. I was stunned to hear someone say it. I was in college then. No one had ever called me an orphan to my face. I can honestly say I never felt unwanted. Never. They wanted "us," not just my adoptive parents, but our other relatives wanted us. They truly did.

Carrie Fisher said, "You're only as sick as your secrets," discussing her memoir, *Wishful Drinking*, on *The Today Show* with Matt Lauer in December 2008.

Yeah, I was sick, sicker than I realized, keeping so many things buried. I knew very little about the "real me." I had no idea as a teenager how much my adoption had actually scarred me. No one said being adopted was an issue. No one said I needed counseling.

Secret Adoption File

One morning, I woke up and decided I needed to do something about opening my adoption records before I left Wisconsin. I walked to the Douglas County Courthouse alone. I was thinking that maybe a sympathetic judge would hear my request in private and let me read my file. It couldn't hurt that I was almost Miss Wisconsin and a University of Wisconsin graduate.

Another word for miracle is "synchronicity." I had miraculously good timing.

Remember, adoptees are not trained genealogists, detectives, or experts in searching for missing persons. I'd kept a newspaper article about a woman, named Florence Fisher, who successfully found, and met, her father. That article gave me hope. Florence went on to found the Adoptee's Liberty Movement Association (ALMA) in New York to assist other adoptees. I wrote to ALMA and put my name and date of birth on their registry. I wanted my medical history and I wanted my name. I wanted to know my ancestry and who my ancestors were. I had a long list. Somehow, Florence Fisher had found her father, and they were reunited. I wanted that, too. If she could do it, I could do it.

I was confused that a birth certificate could list someone as "illegitimate" when it obviously takes two people to conceive a child. *Even if they weren't married, why were they protecting my father's identity?*

By age 22, I had tried the ALMA registry, written a few letters, made some phone calls, but nothing had worked. My mother wasn't trying to find me. That became apparent. I tried calling Catholic Charities (the agency that had handled my adoption) and they treated me like a leper. There was no Internet to consult. I thought I had exhausted all my options. I didn't have papers from my adoption that listed my real name. I had even tried calling hospitals in St. Paul, Minnesota (where I was born), but they said they couldn't help me since their records were sealed, too. I had one last option: the Douglas County Courthouse where they probably had my adoption hearing. They had to know something.

The Judge

I walked into the courthouse in Superior, Wisconsin, and found a judge in his office. I don't know how I chose him, but I did recognize his name (his brother was the principal at my high school). I asked to speak with him in private then explained to him why I was there. Being direct, not pushy, I said I needed my medical information because I was adopted.

The judge explained that adoption files don't usually include medical history (he admitted to me that that wasn't good), and he seemed sincerely interested in what I had to say. I also knew the judge was sizing me up. *Was I mature enough to handle this request and what I was about to get?* Standing there, I tried to disguise my racing mind, to hide the fear and anxiety that he would cause him to say, "No, go away."

I held my breath, composed myself, and asked politely, "Please, sir, let me look at my file. I really need this information," I told him.

He nodded, called someone on the phone, and a woman entered. He told her to retrieve my file. (*God bless this judge!*)

It took a while, of course. I'm sure that there are stacks of adoption files in every courthouse across America, just waiting to be discovered, to expose their secrets. This judge understood and showed his respect for me and my ancestors. This act was at his discretion since adoption files were still sealed in Wisconsin in 2009. His clerk returned and the judge handed me my file, which was a few inches thick. (It was at least two-hundred pages!)

The judge said I could take notes, but that I could not have copies of anything. He gave me a pad and a pencil and told me to take as much time as I needed. I will never ever forget his kindness. I sat alone in his courtroom at a long wood desk. As I read the information on my birth certificate and flipped through page after page, it just didn't seem real. Then it hit me. They were writing about me. I was reading my name for the first time: Laura Jean Thrall.

The name given to me at birth hit me so hard, I couldn't move. I just sat there. Then, quietly, I started to cry. I needed to let it out. But I didn't want the judge to find me crying, so I attempted to compose myself again. There were so many dreary documents about placement and legal forms. I took a few notes on the pad the judge had given me. My hands were shaking. As

I read, my heart swelled. I was getting answers. Prayers were being answered.

I was shocked to read that I was over ten pounds when I was born. I must have been quite a baby and quite a burden. A friend told me later that diabetics have large babies. (My mother died in 2007 from complications of diabetes.) I was struck by the synchronicity that I was the same age as my mother was when she gave me up. I cried for days, even after the shock of what had happened, what I had done, wore off. It was a miracle. I will always be grateful to the judge for letting me read my file. It changed my life.

Chasing Ghosts

"You must know where you came from yesterday, know where you are today, to know where you're going tomorrow." – Cree proverb

I'm over fifty now. I know that my mother, Helen, was 22 when she had me and gave me up. She was not what I expected. Okay, I'm not what I expected.

Getting this life and this experience is no coincidence. This makes me an adoptee uniquely situated. I experienced two worlds growing up, American and Native American, being raised in rural northern Wisconsin. Today, I'm a journalist and write exclusively about Indian Country. I'm good at chasing ghosts.

"But how do I write about Native-American genocide?" I ask Indian friends. They say, "Well, it's not exactly the Holocaust. It's bigger." Genocide, by my definition, means a community of people who were culturally killed, wiped out, or literally erased for political and/or economic reasons. Strong words, but true. Some of us are your next door neighbors. Some of us are not correctly listed on the census. Some of us are Indian only when we look in the mirror.

There are no photos of when early invaders arrived here and began grabbing land, collecting bounties on Indians, or coordinating military massacres. I did not see film footage when a ship pulled up on Turtle Island, but the story lives on. Indians fought long and hard. Tribes did Winter Counts, a kind of Indian census (with additional narrative). Photos and papers exist of Indians signing treaties with white men to enact removals to reservations. I've been to the graveyard for the Wounded Knee Massacre of 1890, the last Indian uprising.

As for the Indian adoption projects, I needed a calculator. If the Native American population was two million, and if just one quarter of all children were removed before the Indian Child Welfare Act of 1978 then, on-paper, 80,000+ children were removed from their families during the early-to-mid-1900s. If the population of American Indians was three million, then over 100,000 babies were removed. I hated this math: 85 percent of children were removed by adoption in 16 states. That's genocide.

I'm Not Giving Up on Any Adoptee

I was contacted by a young woman whose mother, Amy, is an adoptee, born in 1965. They believe Amy is full-blood Hopi and we hope to prove it. Another adoptee, Michael, and I are trying to figure out what language he spoke as a child to give us some clue as to which tribe he might belong to. We believe he's Apache. Another adoptee, Tom, contacted me in 2011 and asked me to help him and his sister find their tribal relatives in Washington State since they were brought to Connecticut and placed in a closed adoption as young children. Tom and his sister believe they might be Colville. I haven't been able to connect them to relatives even though I wrote to a few tribal newspaper editors in Washington and asked for their help.

All of these adoptees come from the Indian Adoption Programs and Projects-era when the US government and the Child Welfare League of America were funding ARENA (Adoption Resource Exchange of North America) and paying churches and agencies to remove Indian children to purposefully place these babies and children with non-Indian parents in closed adoptions.

Since the late 1800s, these adoptions happened before, during, and after residential boarding schools (in the US and Canada). It's no surprise that the numbers of adopted Indian children are calculated in percentages, not actual statistics, and left purposefully vague. (Ontario has a class action suit for adoptees in the works. We know First Nations children were also brought from Canada to the US by way of ARENA.) These two governments decided that assimilation was a very good idea because adoptions far from the reservation would somehow erase the Indian blood and a child's memories of home.

With every phone call I make, I hope to give adoptees something concrete, something helpful, something that will work. In truth, I can't because it doesn't exist, not with sealed adoption records, without paperwork or proof, and current laws that prevent adoptees from knowing their tribal identities.

There are things I want to happen and my list grows after each call for help. First, I want adoptees and families of loss to write to their legislators and tell them that, "This is wrong," until we finally get someone in the government who hears us and offers to help. I want an American government agency to help repatriate adoptees to their tribes. (Canada has three such programs.) I want more people to see this history for what it was: forced assimilation to kill culture in children – a genocide of the mind.

When I get requests from adoptees, I send as many ideas as quickly as I can. If a state (like Kansas or Oregon, for example) has open records, I can guide them to the state agency or registry and then tell them about search angels who will help for free (or for nominal fees). I tell them how to order their adoption files, get court orders, and give examples of how adoptees (like me) got around the laws.

For Amy, Arizona sealed her adoption file. For Michael, New York and New Mexico sealed his adoption files. I want to be able to tell Michael that he is Apache and connect him to his relatives. For Tom and his sister, I want to locate their parents so that we can find out why they were taken as children, but

Washington has sealed both of their adoption records. For all of them, the truth is a mystery.

I want to be able to tell them, "This is what we'll do and it will work. In about a week, you will get a phone call from the tribe and they will help you." But that would be a lie. Now I can only offer them hope.

Finally, I want tribes to do something! Tribes could hire lawyers and legally demand that states and agencies who took children release their names and adoption files. Tribes could create a list of birthdates of children who disappeared, so that adoptees could search for themselves. Tribes could also create some form of welcome ceremony, or reunion powwow, to help the adoptee when he or she meets relatives.

Right now, Native American and First Nation adoptees have mountains to climb, laws to conquer, and no one to turn to. Knowing which tribe can be a huge obstacle when there are over 560 Federally-recognized tribes. For them, it's still "Tribe Unknown."

Adoption conquered and uprooted children and damaged generations of tribal nations. Being adopted ultimately disrupted our rights as sovereign citizens in North America.

Award-winning journalist, **Trace A. DeMeyer**, of Shawnee-Cherokee-French-Canadian-Irish ancestry, is the author of *One Small Sacrifice: A Memoir* that details the little-known history of the Indian Adoption Projects and Indian Child Welfare Act, which includes an account of the jaw-dropping journey to find her father and tribal relatives. A second book (an anthology), *Two Worlds: Lost Children of the Indian Adoption Projects* (co-authored with Patricia Busbee), was published in 2012. Trace's writing has been published in newspapers and journals in The United States, Canada, and Europe. A graduate of the University of Wisconsin-Superior, Trace has received numerous news and feature-writing awards. She lives in Massachusetts. Find her online at *Trace DeMeyer*.

Checking The Bastard Box

WHEN I ARRIVED IN San Francisco, late in the summer of 1996, I had someone else's name. In my bags were packed photographs of someone else's family and every form of ID that I brought with me was fake; my driver's license, all of the credit cards that helped to propel me across the continent, my birth certificate, my Social Security and ATM cards. All fraudulent. My medical records contain no information. My blood type has never been recorded. The person whose name appeared in thick block lettering on my English degree was just as fictitious as the Pucks and Oberons of my undergraduate studies.

I lived in a hotel at the corner of Ellis and Cyril Magnin and fell asleep to the bells clanging on the cable cars coming and going at the Powell Street turnaround two blocks away. I knew no one in San Francisco, let alone California, and the anonymity and distance from the chaos that I left back in New York produced a profound sense of liberation and safety that I had never before experienced in my life. I could not be found, had no obligations to anyone or anything, and had absolutely no history in the state I currently found myself. What I felt then was an immense relief and a certain self-satisfaction in successfully orchestrating the details of my own disappearance.

For over two weeks, I left my room early in the morning and returned after dinner while searching for an apartment (or some other semi-permanent place to live). Somewhere in the midst of all of this running around, I caught a glimpse of a *Chronicle* headline that announced the city's residential occupancy rate had risen to just shy of 100%. I had no concept of the dot-com revolution, could not find Silicon Valley on a map, and had packed a friend's electric typewriter at the last minute as I left my hometown on the East Coast to pursue an MFA in creative writing at San Francisco State University. I was a self-professed Luddite and hadn't thought to factor an impromptu housing crisis into my escape plans. After two weeks of this 9-to-5 schedule, I had two leads on potential living accommodations and neither was really that appealing when it came right down to it. The first was a sliver of a closet space in an artists' co-op at 22nd and Mission that was already bursting at the seams with poets, painters, and other assorted drama queens that would require me to cook for the house on a weekly or bi-weekly basis. The second was a spacious room in one of the famous painted ladies that line Alamo Square Park, but this scenario included a dysfunctional gay couple (one a minister, the other a newly "reformed" go-go boy) and they explicitly prohibited drinking, smoking, and drugs. (I neglected to tell either of these men, at the time, that I found those three things to be unquestionably integral to my own development as a writer.)

Pure luck, and not the multiple agencies that I had registered with, led me to a room that I ended up renting for $375 a month. There was a hand-drawn ad tacked to a board in a Laundromat at Market and Laguna, decorated with flowers and smiley faces, that encouraged me to call a woman who was an interpretive dancer with two recent vacancies in her three-bedroom flat. After a rambling conversation about my housing needs and her plans to study in Spain, I made an appointment to meet her in two days in order to look at the apartment. The next day, however, I happened to be walking by the building and saw a slender woman heading up the stairs. I introduced myself and, after a quick assessment, she let me in to see the flat earlier than expected. The place was huge, disheveled, bright, and cheap, so I jumped at the opportunity to land one of the front bedrooms that boasted bay windows and panoramic views of The Central Freeway and the sex club across the four lanes of Market Street.

I called my friend, Squishy, in Manhattan from a payphone on Fifth Street to tell her the good news. As we were melodramatically screaming at each other about my good fortune, a woman clad in a silver lamé gown, white wings, and a glittery halo rode by on an oversized tricycle built around an actual harp. She smiled at me from her perch several feet above the sidewalk as she rolled by and I took this as a sign that I was, in fact, destined to be there all along. I spent the night at The Gold Dust Lounge near Union Square celebrating my arrival in San Francisco by drinking my weight in Anchor Steam while the Dixieland band further elevated my spirits to heights unimaginable in the weeks prior. Hours before last call I had joined a group of French tourists who were all traveling on the same tacky *rouge, blanc, et bleu* chartered bus and we sang the *Marseillaise* at the top of our lungs that night like a bunch of Gallic Christmas carolers whose calendars were all broken.

The next afternoon, I moved out of the Hotel Gates by making several trips back-and-forth to my new apartment on streetcars from Boston, Chicago, and Los Angeles on the beautiful, and historic, F-Market line. When I was finished, and my easel was set up in the corner of my new room, I thought that I was done. I thought I had accomplished what I had set out to do, which was simply to escape from my own life in Upstate New York and everything that it had entailed – to simply be *away*, untouchable, unreachable. Unfortunately, I could not have been more wrong. Over the next four years, I unpacked my baggage (both literal and metaphorical) as I unraveled publicly, and privately, before finally coming completely undone in the summer just after graduation.

San Francisco, initially, was both a destination and a salve for me as I moved westward. By moving as far away as continentally possible from the complex issues of identity and ownership that I once thought were confined within the city limits of my hometown, I thought that I could resolve problems and vanquish personal demons with geography. By obliterating my own contexts and emotional frames of reference, I had hoped to erase the memories of my fucked-up childhood and violent adolescence, but San Francisco had other plans for me completely. As soon as I thought that I had found my place in the world, the city itself seemed to start questioning my previous affiliations and, at the same time, to categorize me now that I was there. Gay, male, and Caucasian were really the only descriptors that I could bring to the table when I stepped off the Greyhound at the Transbay Terminal and those identifiers, I would come to find out, were not sufficient for me or for the city (over the long haul).

I caught the tail end of the dot comet after completing my degree and worked for a series of Web companies until I was laid off by a series of Web companies. As I scrambled for work in the wake of the burst bubble, I filled out hundreds of applications in dozens of offices and each interview, inadvertently, made me more desperate to know who I was and where the hell I came from. After running the gauntlet of admins and introductions, I would ultimately be left alone with the daunting task of copying all of the information from my résumé onto the prefab corporate forms piled in front of me. Somewhere in this mix, underneath the fields for Social Security Number, Permanent Residence Address, Gender, and Date of Birth, would be the set of boxes that I dreaded most. Regardless of their order, they were invariably introduced by the same innocuous phrase: "Please Check One Only:"

African-American
Non-Hispanic
Filipino
American Indian/Alaskan Native

To live in a city like San Francisco, where every neighborhood has its own separate and distinct ethnic and cultural identity, became a particular version of hell for me (a virtual John Doe).

Chinese
Japanese
Korean
Laotian
Cambodian
Vietnamese

Walking through the crowds on Geary Boulevard at the Nihonmachi Street Fair, chasing the dragons up Grant Avenue and on into Chinatown during the New Year's parade, learning about ugly fruit and *lumpia* in the strange subterranean food court on Columbus, losing hours at Stella Pastry in North Beach staring out the big picture window at all of the people crowding the pavement of the Italian neighborhood, running drunk through the gauntlets of dealers and junkies in The Mission on so many nights with the sounds of Latin *oom-pah-pah!* polkas bouncing out of every open window along Valencia Street, and eating my way through the long provincial city blocks out in the Richmond District one Thai restaurant at a time – All of these things, either wonderful, dangerous, delicious, or some combination thereof, all of them hammered home the fact that I was no one from nowhere. I used to think that my situation was advantageous, that my total inability to be labeled, from within or from without, allowed me to move through life more freely than others. I had always answered with a vague, "I have no idea," when anyone would ask about my background or my family. During these awkward conversations I imagined myself to be an enigmatic *citoyen du monde* who defied categorization solely on the basis of my fiercely independent nature.

>Mexican, Mexican-American, Chicano
>Central American
>South American
>Guamanian
>Hawaiian
>Samoan

I spent innumerable nights drunk and alone in my studio designing a tattoo of a question mark in a font of my own creation. I had always imagined it on my right shoulder, just above my bicep, so that I could offer it up as a silent response to anyone who might inquire about my background by simply rolling up my sleeve. Because there has never been a box to check, or a circle to fill in darkly and completely with a No. 2 pencil, on any form that would allow me to accurately identify, classify, or categorize myself:

>Bastard
>Orphan
>Abandoned
>Unknown

Every block of every neighborhood in San Francisco was a physical reminder of what I was not. I was not Italian, Latin, Asian. I did not speak Spanish, Mandarin, or Tagalog and the only nomenclature that was truly applicable to me at the time were my *genus* and *species*. The politics of identity, with their requisite inclusion by exclusion, seemed to float in with the afternoon fog and work their way into my thoughts, decisions, and dreams more than they had ever before. Rather than being the escapist paradise that I had naïvely envisioned, San Francisco stripped away layer upon layer of scar tissue that had been built up by years of silence, guilt, shame, and institutionally-sanctioned deceit.

I met my mother for the first time when I was thirty and learned that I had actually lived around the corner from her for years while I was in college in New York. She told me things that I was never legally supposed to know such as the names of my grandparents, my younger brother, and of my older sister. Like millions of other American adults raised in adoptive and foster constructs, I do not have legal access to my own immediate or extended family members, medical records, or heritage. My name was changed three times before my tenth birthday and these name changes were (allegedly) meant to convey a sense of inclusion into these new facsimiles of family units. In reality, however, what adoption did in both cases was to simply transfer ownership of a human being from the state to unrelated private citizens upon completion of sizable financial transactions.

Twenty-five years after my past was erased by the State of New York, I stood before a judge in San Francisco Superior Court and took back my own name. I had filed the petition back in March and the first available date for my hearing was 9AM on May 19th, 2003. While I am, by no means, a numerologist I took this as a sign and my heart leapt when the clerk behind the bulletproof glass assigned me the date. I had her repeat it because I thought she might just have been verifying some of the information on the court documents fanned out in front of her. She asked me if I wanted to make my appointment for later that summer after I told her that the nineteenth of May was my birthday.

When I returned for my day in court, I was shaking from too much caffeine and a pent-up frustration resulting from years spent searching for my parents and raging at the machine. For the judge, I'm sure it was just another day at the office as she was calm, cool, and collected when she asked me two simple questions and then sent me on my way. As the focal point of the proceedings, I was damn near twitching and truly unsure if I would actually be able to contain myself once I was face-to-face with a representative of a system that had made so many decisions on my behalf without my input or consent. I had visions of Norma Rae and Erin Brockovich looping through my brain and had half-expected to be dragged from the building while spitting bile and invective at the cogs whose mere presence lent their support to adoption laws and legislation in this country that cause so much pain to so many to this day.

The judge, instead, quietly and confidently returned something to me that had been mine all along. The remainder of my thirty-third birthday was spent in interminable lines at the Department of Motor Vehicles and at the Social Security Administration Office as I started the process of replacing the false papers that I once carried in my wallet with valid forms of ID. At the DMV, I looked directly at the camera, newly sober and born again, and smiled like I had just won the lottery.

Michael Allen Potter is the author of *The Last Invisible Continent: A Memoir* (*Kartografisk Utgaver*). A graduate of The Nonfiction Writing Program at The University of Iowa, Michael was an inmate at the same New York orphanage as Gregory Maguire (of *Wicked* fame), although not concurrently. Find him online at *I, Cartographer*.

Outer Search/Inner Journey

AFTER THE CONDUCTOR'S SHRILL whistle blast, doors closed and the electric train snaked along steel ribbons, rounded a curve and disappeared behind a grove of trees. Surveying the scene, I slowly set the suitcase down without removing my gaze from the surrounding area. I had always considered adoption a mark of inferiority, but had to lock away those feelings during military training because frailty had no place in the life of an infantry officer. Standing alone on the empty dock, I allowed my life-long longing for my mother to slowly emerge. Here in Mörfelden, however, it was safe.

There wasn't a time when I hadn't known that I was adopted. The dreadful realization that I was torn from my mother resulted in a yearning, a primordial ache, to find the woman who had given me life. Every single day, as far back as I could remember, I thought about her and about reestablishing the natural bond that connects mother and child.

As a boy, I learned to live with the suffering and anger of abandonment like someone who slowly disciplines themselves to accept the perpetual pain of a debilitating physical injury. Only by finding my mother could I hope to understand the adoption experience and to find inner peace. In essence, I had never accepted my role as an adopted child (or the life that came with it). I had never felt that I belonged, or that I was accepted by others, or was loved for who I actually was. Emotional serenity was foreign to me, and I believed that healing would only come through reuniting with my mother. I didn't know how, but I was certain that she would have the answers to some of my oldest questions. *Why did she give me away? Where do I come from? Where do I belong? Is there anyone who looks like me? Who am I?* These thoughts haunted me constantly.

The search was more than a simple journey to find my mother. It was also a voyage of inner faith. I felt that if I could find out who my mother was, then I would find out who I was. By discovering my German mother, I would accept my role in life, become capable of receiving and giving love, and gain a sense of belonging.

Standing on the railroad platform at Mörfelden, I grasped for the first time the reality that I might actually find her. It felt strange after so many years of wishful thinking and hope to realize that my dream might just come true. A separate part of me awakened at the same time to question my search. The questioning voice was *reason* and it came to challenge the inborn bond that linked me to my mother. For the first time, I had doubts about my desire to find her. *Did I truly want to?*

Reason asked: What, if any, positive outcome might result from a successful search? Wasn't it enough to appreciate life as an adoptee and to enjoy the many gifts I'd been given? *Reason* went on to compare the life of an adoptee with that of an orphan. In all categories – wealth, education, opportunities – an adoptee came out ahead, and it (logically) followed that a second set of parents were far better than none.

Sentiment came forward and offered a different point of view: *Reason's* evaluation was based only on material criteria and failed to recognize emotion. The origins of human behavior often begin with the invisible stirrings of feelings. *Sentiment* said that a child could grow up in the house of the wealthiest family in the world, attend the very best schools and be given every available material gift, but that that would never be enough. Without love, a child will remain forever incomplete. If love was the chief criterion on which to evaluate life, *sentiment* viewed a penniless orphan, who knew love, as better off than a loveless adopted child surrounded with mountains of riches.

Reason countered and asked a different question, one designed to stop my search: By simply finding my mother, how would my life as an adoptee change? After all, what difference would it really make? Why not simply bury the past and get on with life?

Instinct stepped in to respond: Adoptive parents can never claim that they are the natural parents. This biological chasm, which cannot be bridged, has special significance for adopted children regarding their mothers. The unseen bond that forever connects mother with child (that originates in the womb), is a link that doesn't exist between adopted children and their adopted mothers. When this link is broken, it shatters the natural order of life. When separated, an inherent reaction is for a mother and her lost offspring to search for one another.

Reason again objected. Hurling a series of "what ifs," *reason* suggested that a successful search could do more harm than good. *What if she rejected me a second time? What if she was an impoverished old maid? What if my sudden reappearance had a detrimental impact on her? What if she was dead?*

Curiosity answered the last of *reason's* challenges: adopted children usually don't look like their adopted parents. That was certainly true in my case. I yearned to find my own flesh and blood, to see someone who looked like me. I wanted to know about my family, where we came from, and something about our history. I wanted to know why I wasn't kept by my parents and, instead, put into an orphanage. My mother would answer these questions, I assumed. The urge to discover her outweighed any fear of possible rejection. I didn't care what she looked like, where she came from, or what her position in life might be. I simply had to know and *curiosity* drove me to search.

Reason, defeated, was left to admit the human condition included more than what could be compartmentalized within the confines of rational thought. Emotions fall outside of the scope of logic and are unknowable to reason. *Sentiment*, *instinct*, and *curiosity* were real, although they defy the five physical senses. My arrival in Mörfelden was proof of the bond connecting mother and child, because I had no logical basis for being there. Conquering doubt, I returned to the task at hand and stepped off of the platform.

Peter Dodds was born to German parents and later adopted by a couple from the United States. His memoir, *Outer Search Inner Journey*, is the first book written by a foreign-born adoptee on the subject of international adoption. Peter proudly served as an Army officer and Ranger, directed an international program for The United States Olympic Committee, and worked as a member of a legislative staff. In addition to earning a master's degree, Peter is also a graduate of The International Olympic Academy in Greece. As a leader in the growing movement to reform international adoption, Peter is committed to changing the system so that removing children from their homelands is always done in the best interest of the child and only as a "last resort." He is an international speaker and has delivered keynote addresses at adoption conferences in New Zealand and in Canada. Find him online at *Peter F. Dodds*.

What's It Like to Be "Adopted?"

WHAT'S IT LIKE TO be adopted? It's lonely and it can be debilitating (if you let it). It's confusing, frustrating, and it can seriously screw with you emotionally, physically, and psychologically.

For me, the experience of being adopted was both positive and negative (especially in my formative years). Attitudes in the 1960s, I think, dictated how the people who adopted me chose to deal with the fact of me being from a different race and culture. It was a subject that we did not talk about. I was the elephant in the room. As a child, I was curious. As I grew up, I become more and more curious. I pushed to know more. *Who was I?* **What** *was I?* But my adoptive parents refused to field my questions. Silence and reprimand were their stock answers. It has taken many years of therapy and personal soul searching to get where I am today. I have found a balance of sorts, a contentment and understanding of who and what I am, (or rather what I am not). Let me make it perfectly clear that I am profoundly grateful for having been adopted. If I hadn't, I would not be addressing you as I do now. I certainly would not have become the person that I am or have a professional life in the arts. Having said that, I do not (as many other Chinese adoptees that I have encountered in the UK) feel beholden. I was extremely lucky that the therapist that I went to very early on taught me that I did not have to feel guilty, that I didn't have to feel beholden to the family that adopted me, that I did not *owe* them anything – that I should take control of my life. As an adult, I no longer had to put up with decisions that had been taken on my behalf, which had isolated and *deformed* my identity. It sounds easy in the cold light of day but, like many people in recovery, it proves to be the most difficult and elusive thing to do – to take control. I was so used to being told what to think, how to behave, and how to feel that having freedom as an adult was worse than being confined and restricted as a child. It took a long while for me to understand the nature of my predicament.

I have had to fight my way through silence, prejudice, and out-and-out racism from a very early age. Having been abused at infant school by the incumbent school bully, to the institutionalised racism which sadly still creeps along the corridors of industry (even now in the 21st century) in supposedly multicultural Britain. I have had to come to terms with the fact that as someone who looks, for all intents and purposes, to be "Chinese," I am (and always will be) *incomplete*. The loss of my mother tongue and of my cultural heritage marked me in the Chinese-speaking community as someone to be wary of. Someone not to be trusted. Someone not Chinese.

It is something that I think I will always silently mourn.

To those from the indigenous Caucasian community, I was an outsider. A foreigner. The *other* to be feared, to be abused, to be kept at bay. The reasons for not being able to connect with my own culture and language are many and varied. The clean-break attitude was considered the best approach at the time.

Now there is no excuse (or reason!) why a transracially-adopted child cannot retain cultural and linguistic links until such time as they reach their majority (at which point they may decide to set aside such matters). At least they will have the basic tools to be able to communicate in their own language, should they ever feel the need to do so.

My job as an actor is all about communication. It is odd to think that I have spent most of my adult life feeling culturally and linguistically dislocated. It is also odd that I chose a profession where I would be literally on display, but I personally have seen this as choosing to hide in plain sight. When I was younger, the feelings of rejection and of inadequacy (fueled by the embarrassment at not being able to respond to a fellow countryman that was followed closely by the looks of suspicion and mistrust) hit me very hard. It was deeply upsetting and had long-lasting, and devastating, effects on me.

I did not have the advantage of the World Wide Web or other opportunities to learn that are now available. I am neither pro-, nor anti-, transracial adoption, but I would say that transracial adoption should be the absolute last resort. I would like to see the West investing in the Third World to improve their own domestic adoption systems to ensure that children remain in their country of origin. Identity is a strange beast, completely overlooked and taken for granted by those who do not have to question who, or what, they are in society. But for those of us who cannot benefit from the reflection of society's mirror re-enforcing our physiognomy, it is elusive, making us wander a no man's land between two cultures, two lineages, and two distinct "what might have beens."

Take it from one who has trodden that road. As parents, we have the onerous responsibility of equipping our children with all the tools to deal with life, including the unsavoury and the negative. I would hope that in this age of information that, if a family decided to transracially adopt a child, that he or she would not be kept in the dark about where they came from, that they would be taught their mother-tongue and get to know their culture and heritage in depth. (And I am not referring to a cursory Sunday school that teaches children a few traditional songs by rote or does a few collages about the Moon Festival.)

I was adopted into a Britain that is very different from the one that I now inhabit. It was emerging from the austerity of the postwar years. The race riots of Notting Hill had only just died down. Notices hanging in the windows of rooms to let stating, "No Irish, No Dogs, and No Blacks" had not long been taken down. When the infamous "Rivers of Blood" speech by the Tory MP (Member of Parliament) was delivered on April the 11th, 1968, I had been in the country but five years. There were no laws, civil or otherwise, to prevent discrimination based on colour or ethnicity. If you were black, the "n" word was used freely in public by anti-immigrationists. As a person who looked Chinese, I was constantly spat at and verbally abused, called "Chink," and told to go back home. On one occasion, I was physically attacked in broad daylight. I suffered three broken ribs, a cracked cheekbone, and two very blackened and bruised eyes. I couldn't understand why no one had intervened. Today, that verbal abuse is returning to the streets in Britain, but this time, it's coming out of the mouths of second- and third-generation South Asians (both Bangladeshi and Pakistani). This is deeply troubling and truly disheartening.

I was not given the choice of whether or not I retained my Chinese name, whether I was taught to speak Chinese, or whether I would learn about Chinese culture or heritage. It is something that, for many, many years, left a gap in my being and in my identity. It is something that I still have not come to terms with. I am who I am. Incomplete as I am, I am now whole. I am proud to be who I am – a child of both the East and of the West. It has been a long and difficult road, one that I would not wish on even my worst enemy.

In spite of the challenges of being Chinese and transracially adopted, I have survived both physical and mental abuse. And I have prevailed. The challenges that I encountered as a child (the bullying, the prejudice, and the racism), have made me who I am today.

We must further assist any future generations of transracially-adopted children (if society persists with this practice). The West must make these children's transitions into other worlds and alternative cultures easier.

There is no doubt that I would not be here if the history of Hong Kong had not been so tied up with Great Britain. Hong Kong would not be the Special Administrative Region of China that it is today had the British not taken it as a Crown Colony.

I occupy a space in UK society that very few people do. I am neither one thing nor the other. Accepted by neither the British nor recognised by some British-Chinese as being Chinese. I feel like a ghost, invisible to the culture and society that brought me here, but also invisible to the community and culture of my birth. My heritage and the cultural umbilical cord having been severed at birth by transracial adoption – an act perceived to be responsible for saving my life.

Made in Hong Kong and exported to the United Kingdom in the 1960s as a transracial adoptee, **Lucy Sheen** is a writer, filmmaker, and author who modestly refers to herself as a dyslexic actor. She loves Dim Sum, Yorkshire pudding, and green tea. Trained at The Rose Bruford College of Speech and Drama, Lucy graduated in 1985 with Honors with a BA in Theatre Arts. She created a theatre production called "There are Two Perfectly Good Me's: One Dead, the Other Unborn," in which she explores the consequences of a British family's adoption of a Chinese baby. The impetus for this work is to give voice to the matter of race and intercountry adoption after only finding "stereotypical clichéd characterizations of what people think East Asians are or should be."

The Korean Drop

HAVE YOU EVER HEARD of "Chinese water torture?" This is a process whereby a small drop of water is repeatedly aimed towards the same place on the victim's forehead. Each drop in itself is not painful, but over time, since the drops hit the same spot over and over – the pain becomes unbearable. The systematic landing on one area only is the reason it is called *torture* as opposed to "only pain." That's how I see my Korean adoptee experience. I guess it could be called "Korean water torture," instead.

My name is Sunny Jo, but it hasn't always been my name. I was adopted from South Korea to Norway when I was a year old. I was ripped away from everything familiar to me. Rice and kimchi were exchanged for meatballs and potatoes, and morning calm for midnight sun. In a single moment, my path was changed forever and I can never go back or pretend it never happened.

I grew up as an only child. My Norwegian parents accepted me as their own and tried their best to raise me as a "normal" Norwegian child. I grew up with the Norwegian culture as my only point of reference, I was fluent in the language, and I had an all-Norwegian name. That I was Norwegian was just the way things were, no questions asked.

And my adoptive parents were so happy for having me, I was their solution to infertility, but that does not mean I have ever doubted their love or their acceptance for me. I was their "daughter" from day one. I never lacked anything. Through my arrival, they got a child and, as a result, the family they were dreaming about. *Since most people have had individual "drops" fall on them occasionally in life, few truly understand the pain caused by constant dripping.*

Due to the fact that Norway has amongst the highest, per capita, number of Korean adoptees in the world, I was never the only KA around. "Everyone" knew someone who was (or had adopted) from Korea. Growing up as a Korean adoptee in Norway probably saved me from much of the racism and stereotyping that other immigrants experienced.

There was, however, a downside. As a result of the assumed benefits which I received from living a privileged and affluent life in Norway, people often pointed out how "lucky" I was for these opportunities. I was told that I should feel grateful for being adopted. More than once was I patted on the cheek by an old, well meaning lady who told me how cute "my kind" were and asked me (with pity in her voice) if people had been nice to me. And both adults and children alike took the opportunity to remind me of the poverty and despair which existed abroad, and how privileged I was for getting to grow up in Norway. At the same time, they would highlight that I was Norwegian, and not an immigrant (like the Vietnamese refugees or the Pakistani guest workers), once again emphasizing how "lucky" I was for being here. *To me, rainfall or falling in a body of water causes discomfort, even danger, which might be fatal in the end, BUT it does not cause the intense pain felt from the "drop." One of the most painful aspects of the "drop" is that there is no escape from it. In other words, I am forced to live forever with the drop, which is both trivialized and (often) invisible to the people around me.*

As a result of Norwegian society's attitudes towards what was considered "foreign," I internalized the values and ideas which told me that life anywhere other than in Norway would have been inferior. My adoptive parents had been told by the adoption agency that I would not have had any chances for a decent life if I had remained in South Korea. So, being adopted was my only chance at happiness, and that I ended up in Norway was considered to be my lucky draw in life.

With the ideals of social equality and global solidarity being dominant, and the self-proclaimed open-mindedness of the supposedly "colour blind" majority, I grew up thinking that race and ethnicity did not matter. What they considered to be important was the fact that someone loved me and that the highly-valued benefits of education and democracy were within my reach. And, for a long time, I believed these myths. After all, everyone meant well, and I was made to feel guilty if I questioned their good intentions.

Still, it just never felt right. It took years before I could put the forbidden, difficult feelings into words, the feelings that I had not even dared to acknowledge even to myself. There simply was no room for my loneliness and feelings of alienation (as all the space was consumed by the happiness of my parents and society's colour-blind conviction of having done "something good" by "saving" me). To show anything but gratitude and satisfaction would be like slapping the faces of the adoptive parents, who loved me, and the people who had accepted me as one of them. So I carried my pain alone, wearing a mask for fear that I might destroy someone else's illusion.

I know that no one will ever understand the torture (and, yes, in many ways being a KA has been emotional TORTURE), without having experienced it themselves. I know that it will always be viewed as less painful than many of its alternatives (by those who have not felt the pain themselves), to the point of being denied. But that will NEVER take away the pain of my lived experiences and feelings, nor will it make me feel grateful for being saved from the "worse alternative." My focus is to stop both the drip and the alternatives and, from that starting point, one kind of suffering is not more acceptable because it is "better" than the others.

Only as an adult could I put my feet on the soil I had left as an infant. Instead of a poverty-stricken Korea where people were struggling to put food on the table, I encountered a modern country that lacked nothing in material. Most importantly, though, I saw the viable alternatives to the life I had lived. I met the children who, for various reasons, could not grow up in their own families, but who were given a new chance in their own country. There, right in front of me, were the domestic opportunities which, I had been told all my life, did not exist. Instead of lives filled with misery, I met thriving vibrant people who never had to leave Korea, despite their unfortunate circumstances. And I envied them with my entire being.

When I was 24, I met my Korean parents and lived in their house (which answered the question about what my life would have been if I had not been adopted). My younger sister (who grew up with our parents), always had food on the table, had all of her material needs met, and got a higher education. I found out the real reason why I was adopted out, and the sense of loss I felt is indescribable. Without my parents' approval, my entire life was altered when my future was stolen by a kidnapper. And I realized that all my suffering had been for nothing because it never had to happen!

Not a day goes by without grief for the losses I suffered because of a long chain of events which eventually led to me growing up so far away from Korea. Every single day I live with the consequences, separated from my own family, not only by geography, but also by language, culture, and mindset. And when I look at my Korean sister, living her life like the way mine should have been, I feel a sting in my heart, not only because I could have had it, but because I am supposed to feel lucky because I didn't (and because my adoptive parents' lifestyle, by many, is considered to be superior to that of my

Korean parents). To be "saved" from drowning only to live the rest of my life with this incessant drop, I would have preferred to not be pulled out in the first place. In a way, it is kind of like the analogy of a transplanted organ – The organ will forever be foreign tissue.

When I'm asked if I believe in adoption, I answer that I do. *Why?* Because I believe that adoption has a place and, if handled correctly, it can be a positive alternative for children who cannot remain in the care of their own families. I believe that the pain inflicted by the initial separation can be healed by loving, understanding adoptive parents and that adopted children can thrive if their new family is carefully prepared for the upcoming challenges.

I do not, however, think that adding the additional burdens of being separated from one's parents, country of birth, culture of origin, and language to grow up in racial and ethnic isolation should ever be inflicted upon a child. Losing your own family is more than enough to handle. The price paid is simply too big, and no amount of "acceptance" or material wealth can ever make up for the losses involved.

Instead, I encourage domestic solutions and I have, with my own eyes, seen them in action in Korea and elsewhere. Exponentially more resources should be spent on family preservation, as most families would have kept their children if they had only been given a fair chance. Secondly, domestic adoption (or other placements in local communities) should be encouraged, e.g. through SOS Children's Villages. Unlike orphanages, SOS Villages consist of families with full-time, stay-at-home "parents" in charge of a family house (located in a cluster of similar family houses). The children grow up with siblings and friends, meaning that they will never be "the only one" of their race, ethnic group, or circumstance. The children go to local schools and they have "normal" lives. The best part is that they get to remain in their own country, to keep their own names, and do not have to be uprooted from their native cultures. So, in the event that they one day can be reunited with their parents, there will be no culture shock or language barriers to further separate them.

Those things might seem trivial to most people, but they would have meant the world to me. At the same time, I know that such opinions are not popular with those who think of themselves as "colourblind" and tolerant. *I feel like a stolen heart from a corpse trapped in a foreign body. Drip. Drop. Drip. Drop. There is no bigger pain than the one that is widely considered a blessing.*

Sunny Jo was born in South Korea, but after being kidnapped from her family as an infant, she was adopted to Norway and given a new name and "official" paperwork. She grew up as an only child but learned that she had a younger sister and an older brother (who was kidnapped at the same time, but instead adopted to the United States) when she located, and reunited with, her Korean family in 2000. Sunny has lived in different countries around the world and currently lives in Stockholm, Sweden, with her cats. She is an adoptee activist and writer who published a memoir, *From Morning Calm to Midnight Sun*, in 2005.

Waiting for My Next Adoption

THIS IS DEDICATED TO all people in the world who have had to be adopted or who feel they have been mistreated (and to the people who are in any way connected with this problem).

My Childhood

Born in 1966 in a small New Hampshire town, god knows where, I was the child of god knows whom. The stories I've heard about my folks leave most things to the imagination. Until the age of six, practically no human being has any memories, except for those few very outstanding experiences. I had a couple of these experiences that I'll never forget. When I was about three months old, I saw myself strapped in a car seat watching my parents waving goodbye. It was a white International Scout. The driver of the truck looked angry. A very old and musky type of smell that one has to get used to very quickly otherwise one will feel a strong attack of nausea. Having no one to tell me who I was or where I came from, I found myself asking myself who I actually was. *Was I just another product of the Woodstock baby boom, another face to feed, another "war child," another number? Who knew and who cared?*

My Memories

When I was six, I had a bicycle accident while one of my sisters was trying to teach me how to ride. She wasn't the smartest kid in the world, so she said, "Because we're both not very strong, we'll use the hill." This hill was a fairly steep one with four sharp turns that had just been paved. I pushed the bike out on the driveway and got on. To my surprise, she got on as well. She pushed off, not telling me where the brakes were or how they worked. You can imagine a six-year-old kid trying to balance and steer a bicycle for the first time, heading into a curve and down a 45-degree hill with trees on one side and a creek on the other. To make a long story short, I found myself in the creek in a matter of seconds with the bicycle on my chest and my sister across my legs.

The Hospital

After screaming for help for what seemed like an eternity, someone finally came. Going to the emergency room was imperative. I left the hospital practically covered in bandages and was not able to use my hands for a month.

The Truth

The second significant memory had a big emotional impact. One day, I was feeling particularly confused. My brothers and sister told me that I was "no kin of theirs," so I went to my mom to find out what they meant.

"Mom, can we talk? Rob, Chuck, and Susie are trying to tell me that I'm no family of theirs. Why are they being so mean to me? I'm part of the family too, aren't I?" I asked.

"Well, I guess it really is time for us to talk. What they said is indeed true," Mrs. Zack replied.

"How can you say something like that?" I cried out in shock.

Trying to soothe me, she replied, "The answer I have to give you may be a very difficult thing for you to deal with." She was busy cooking in the kitchen.

"Where's dad?" I interrupted her, angrily.

"Their father lives in Florida and I can't tell you where your parents are. All I know is that I have to take care of you until someone comes for you. I don't even know who your parents are."

Mrs. Zack ran into the other room after I confronted her. I stayed where I was, crying and desperate for more answers, for hours on end, I ignored the call for dinner (even though she was making macaroni and cheese). After what seemed like forever to me, Mrs. Zack brought me some food. I ignored it. Then she said, "Look, I'm sorry I had to tell you that way, but that was the only way I knew how. The people who brought you to me weren't very clear in their reasons. Besides, I've already told you too much. I was supposed to refer you to them when you asked me questions like that."

Angrily, I replied, "If you can't tell me more than that, call them now, 'cause I want some answers. By the way, who are these people and why don't I know them?" I got up, grabbed the plate, and ran to my room, where my favorite "brother" was studying. Wanting to talk, I asked Rob if he knew anything.

My Confusion

Rob sounded pretty fed up, "Can't you just..." but when he saw that I was crying, he put his book down and asked, "What's the matter? Are you OK? Did someone hit you or something?"

I cried, "You knew all the time, didn't you? Why didn't you tell me? You were the only one I really trusted. I mean, you're not really my brother."

Rob looked shocked and put me on his lap. "I'm sorry, but I'm not allowed to talk to you about that. I thought you were here for keeps. Did mom just tell you that you have to leave or something like that?"

I slapped Rob and ran away. Because of the bike accident and the discussion with Mrs. Zack, I suddenly felt that there was no one I could trust. In a state of anger, disappointment, and total confusion, I tried to find a place to hide.

My Hiding

Not wanting to be found by anyone, I wandered through the night. After a couple of hours of wondering if anyone was trying to find me, I saw the police and a couple of so-called family members. I hid away in a ditch in some bushes that stuck me in the back and neck. After an hour or two of hiding, I heard one of the police officers call off the search because it was too dark. Since I felt I couldn't trust anyone, I double-checked what I just heard by sticking my hand out to confirm my situation. No one saw my hand. Feeling hungry, angry, and tired, I looked for a place to sleep for the night.

But there in those thorny bushes in the middle of the night, I just didn't know what to do with myself. I left the ditch and ended up in a junkyard. Fearing that it might rain, I checked some cars to see if they were unlocked. I finally found one that opened, climbed into the back seat, and fell asleep.

My respite was short-lived, though. Suddenly I woke up, scared. I had the feeling that something was staring down at me. I thought I heard the "thing" tell me that it would come back to see me. Whether this was true or not, I'm still not really sure. It was some kind of paranormal experience. Before I knew it, I was back in the house that I had run away from, a place that I now had the feeling that no one cared that I had been gone.

My School

A couple of weeks later, I was in the family car being driven to school. I had the feeling that the family was going to abandon me again, like my parents had already done. I didn't say a word for the whole ride, which seemed never-ending. Once at school, only the teacher spoke to me (and that was to get my name for attendance). Even though I was surrounded by children, I felt totally alone for the rest of the day. Because I was at school, and out of that boring house, time seemed to fly by. I was in the same school as some of the other members of the family, but again it seemed as if no one would talk to me. I really felt like some kind of outcast.

The Dinner

One evening at the dinner table one of my adoptive brothers, Chuck, said, "I don't want anyone at school to know that he lives with us. Nobody likes him and I don't want anything to do with him because it took me long enough to build up the friendships I have."

Mrs. Zack scolded, "Listen you, we all have to live together because we are a family and that includes your little brother. For now."

"But," Chuck tried to say.

"But, nothing," Rob interrupted. "I didn't like the fact that you were in the same school as me either, when you first got there, but I had to accept that because we both have to eat and sleep in the same house. It would only make things worse if there was some problem at school."

Days later, one of my adoptive sisters called me from the end of the hall at school, walked up to me, and led me outside.

Chuck was talking to some friends of his and called us over.

"You guys already know Sally, this is my foster brother. I heard you were going to mess with him. Don't!" Chuck said to everyone in the area.

From that moment on, it seemed like everyone knew me and accepted me. I was pleasantly surprised. But something still bothered me. *Why was Chuck being so nice to me all of a sudden?* In the whole family, Chuck seemed to like me the least. *Was he up to something?*

A couple of months into this popularity and it became clear to me (or so I thought). Chuck had been spending most of his recesses talking to a girl. It seemed as if he had feelings for her, I concluded.

The Threat

But, as it transpired, my conclusion was incorrect. One night, I woke up and felt him playing with my private parts. I was horrified. *What is this asshole doing on my bed at this time of night and what is he doing?* I tried to push him away, but he was too big. I tried to call Rob, but he was asleep wearing headphones, as usual. I really didn't know what to think. All I knew was that because he was being so secretive about it, it couldn't be good. While he tried to brainwash me into thinking that it was normal and kind of cool, I felt ashamed, scared, and confused. This went on for many nights. *When will someone catch wind of what he was doing to me?*

As time went by, each encounter got more-and-more obscene. One night, I was grounded a week for grabbing a snack out of the refrigerator when it was meant for dinner. Chuck also got sent to our room for talking back. I thought he did that on purpose so he could get at me again. (In the bedroom, there were two bunk beds and one single bed, five beds in all. I slept on the bottom of one of the bunk beds, Chuck slept on the top of the other, and Rob slept in the single bed.)

That day, Chuck came upstairs laughing and crying at the same time. I had heard him yelling at Mrs. Zack, so I didn't ask him what had happened. He studied for a while and then turned around and stared at me. We talked for a while. In fact, I was surprised that we talked for so long, but then it happened. He told me that he would *kill* me if I told anyone what he was doing. He continuously repeated this threat until he was certain I understood him.

"Why are you doing this to me?"

His only answer was to do it again. It wouldn't help to scream. I had no choice but to let it happen. The terror from these experiences created emotional scars that I still carry.

We heard the front door slam shut when Rob got home. Chuck and I knew that he would make a sandwich for himself then come upstairs to study or to work on one of his model planes, a hobby of his that often kept him busy all day. Fortunately, Chuck stopped what he was doing and went to his own bed, signaling to me that I should act like I was asleep. Rob saw that we were both in our beds, trying to sleep. But I noticed that Rob kept looking at me, as if he suspected something. I tried to signal to him but Chuck saw me instead of Rob. Chuck made the gesture of a knife slicing his throat. So scared, I immediately stopped trying to get Rob's attention. Until the call for dinner, the rest of the evening slowly and silently ticked by. At dinner no one said a thing. I was kind of hoping that someone would start a loud conversation with someone else, so that I could tell Mrs. Zack what was happening, but had no such luck.

The Game

After dinner I took a shower. The shower was connected to the girls' bedroom. I had to wear a pair of pajamas to go to my bedroom. Sally, one of my foster sisters, was waiting for me. She indicated that she wanted to play a game with me. We both sat down quietly in the effort to not to disturb Mrs. Zack. We both knew that if she came upstairs she would tell us to go to bed and then wait by the door until she was convinced that we were really asleep. The game that Sally wanted to play was just as kinky as the "games" Chuck played with me. I thought, *What is this family's obsession with my genitals?*

The Visitor

After a couple of months of isolation, Mrs. Zack came upstairs to tell me that there was a social worker downstairs. I wet my pants, that's how scared I was. All kinds of thoughts went through my mind: *Am I finally going to find the answers to my questions? Am I finally going to be rescued from the horror of this house? Are my parents asking for me? Is Mrs. Zack fed up with me?* I was filled with fear, curiosity, and hope for a better situation while I changed my pants.

Standing in the living room was the same man who took me away from my parents.

"Are you going to take me back home?" I asked, excited.

"No," the man told me. "I have better news for you. I have a couple outside who want to adopt you."

I didn't know what to think.

"You will spend a day with them and tell me what you think of them this evening," he commanded.

I said, "I have a lot of questions for you. Do you have any answers for me? Mrs. Zack was supposed to call you about all the questions I had. Did she do that?"

"Yes, she did, but we don't have any time to talk about that now. The couple is waiting for you outside. Get some toys, or whatever, and let me introduce you to them."

The Couple

I spent the afternoon with the couple. The woman was young, but the man seemed a lot older. He had a huge beer gut. They were very nice, though, extremely generous, and we seemed to get along fairly well. After a few hours, we met with the social worker again. We decided to spend the summer together and then report back to him. I agreed (mainly because of the hell I was going through with Chuck). After saying a very quick "goodbye" to the Zacks, I followed the couple home. On the way to their house, we stopped for dinner. I ate so much that I didn't want any dessert, which they found very strange for a nine-year-old boy. The woman decided to get something a little closer to home. Once in New Jersey, where they lived, I agreed to dessert and spotted a Baskin-Robbins ice cream parlor. The man told me that he'd stop if I could pronounce it correctly. After numerous attempts and some tears (because I had an accent that I couldn't unlearn in a matter of minutes), he stopped. I must admit that I gorged myself, but that was fine with the man since it appeared as if he wanted me to be just as heavy as he was!

I spent a very fun summer with these people. We went to the beach, had picnics, and went to a zoo, but something I'll never forget happened there. The lady and I were riding an elephant (of all things) and she had me sit behind her on the enormous animal. Being small, I had to hold onto her. With every bump the elephant made I felt my hands being pushed up-and-down. The moment she saw her husband, she pushed my hands away. This type of thing went on for the whole summer. The man started to get irritated. At the end of the summer, he fished up an excuse not to take me as their "son" and I was gone.

Another Adoption

I spent a month or two with the family back in New Hampshire. They showed me pictures of myself when I was an infant, playing with a toy that I remembered. They said they had taken care of me before. They wanted to adopt me, but had chosen another boy. Hearing that excuse, I felt like even more of an outcast. The first real signs of depression settled in. After a few fights with the other boy, I was off again.

After four months in another house, the social worker visited again. "Write me a paper with your idea of the ideal parents and a list of things you would like to do with them," he stated.

"You still don't have any answers for me do you?" I asked.

"Got to go," the social worker said before delivering the following news, "I have a candidate for you. Do you mind if it's a single male?"

I kicked him off of the farm. "All I want is some answers."

A week passed by and he came back. I gave him the paper he had asked for and, a couple of days later, he came to wish me good luck because, "A single man is on his way to come and get you."

So, I sat and waited for my next adoption.

Bob Honecker was adopted at the age of ten by a physically- and sexually-abusive single man. After 46 years of not knowing if his parents were dead or alive, Bob Honecker found them in the summer of 2013. During the visit with his mother, he learned that she was forced to put him up for adoption. Devastatingly, Bob learned that his father had passed away within days of potentially reuniting with him. Bob is currently married and works as a caregiver, along with his wife, and he became a Certified Peer Support Worker in 2013 (the same year he reunited with his mother). After all the challenges and trauma Bob has faced, his purpose is to build a more humane world. He says, "Logic is a tool for survival as people are overwhelmed by emotions." His Facebook Group is: "U.N.A U're Not Alone."

PART 3: *Abandoned*

Iron Bed

Jolting awake during the night,
Wet legs, wet sheets, candy-striped,
Glass door allows shafts of light,
That spotlight the corner and my plight.

Outside is the bathroom of this old house
Where Tom, the prowler, lurks and peeps.
Going out there is not an option,
So I lie in the dark, damp, with the creeps.

All alone in this crumbling wreck,
Empty attics and cellars, with leaks and creaks,
Locked up tight in this one good room,
Safe for the moment, but I spoke too soon.

"Water breaking," Mum would say
To her friends, in a whispered way.
I sit up straight, trembling, groaning,
"I have to move, the baby is coming."

Lack of knowledge was not of my making
Mrs. Haylock prevented my prenatal learning.
"It's not for you, dear," she said with a sneer,
"It's just for the married, are we quite clear?"

Belly aching, speeding across town,
Swiftly dressed in an old hospital gown,
Shaved and given an enema, very quick.
"Here's a mask, breathe deeply when you see fit."

All day I watched the clouds drift away,
Through the large windows (sixteen panes, I'd say),
Until I reached down and felt a small head,
"I think I need help," I called from my bed.

I was whisked to a theatre, many people arrived.
It seemed I was an unlikely prize,
"A teaching opportunity," they said as they gathered,
Not for me, I could see, as I was firmly tethered.

My legs were put into great steel stirrups
A sheet was hung from a pole 'cross my middle.
"Just do this," "Just do that," "No, don't do that,"
"Leave that sheet where it is, you are not to meddle."

He was softly mewing and squirming about,
On my right thigh, I could feel him alright.
"Let me have him," I said, as I pulled down that sheet,
"Take him away," she demanded, without losing a beat.

I know now what I didn't know when,
God's police were in charge, held the reins then.
I love my boy, and he loves me,
But the stolen years never let me be.

Darelle Duncan

Immaculate Deceptions

"The bond between a mother and her child is naturally sacred. It is physical, psychological and spiritual. It is very resilient and very flexible. It can stretch very far – naturally. Any artificial or violent injury to this 'stretch' constitutes a serious psychic trauma to both mother and child – for all eternity." – *Mothers on Trial: The Battle for Children and Custody*, Phyllis Chesler, 1986

MANY MOTHERS ARE JUST starting to learn the truth that the adoption industry is responsible for the destruction of natural families and that their government, to save money by keeping single mothers off welfare, owns its own share of the blame. They know, too, that in an effort to professionalize their careers, social workers invented their own "cure" for "unwed motherhood," revising it over the years to suit their needs and purposes. But the cure always required the pressured surrender of babies by unprotected mothers to the adoption industry in numbers never seen before or since the 1950s.

Myths:

- That's just the way adoption was back then.
- Adoption is a wonderful, loving thing. Your child deserved a better life. You were too young to raise a child.
- Social workers tried to help you, not hurt you. They help society.

Facts:

- The separation of mother and child should *never* have occurred (regardless of the era). The mother and child bond is the most sacred. Mothers are *real* mothers regardless of age or income and have the right to raise their own children. They need support, guidance, and encouragement, not condemnation and banishment.
- Adoption is the intentional amputation of a family member. It is family violence. It is never wonderful or loving. Children deserve the life, and the mother, that nature intended for them.
- Social workers did *not* help. They profoundly hurt countless mothers and their children. No one should ever play God with other people's lives.

Mothers are learning how social workers and society cared much more about the wants (not needs) of the increasing number of infertile, married couples who were demanding "families." Today, this realization that social workers used *a vulnerable mother's* baby to resolve that "want" and "need," while ignoring the natural mother's entitlement, as well as all legal protections available to her, justifiably generates anger. A mother's need, her right, is to keep her own baby regardless of her age, marital status, or income.

It is shocking to learn, in light of today's atmosphere of personal rights and protections, that, according to such sources as the Associated Press ("Unwed Mom Recalls Forced

Sterility," Bill Baskervill, May 2002), *The Richmond Times-Dispatch* ("US Focus: Hidden History, Sterilized by The State, North Carolina Gave Great Power to Eugenics Panel," Kevin Begos, Media General, and Peter Hardin (*Times-Dispatch*, Washington), December 2002) and *The Los Angeles Times* ("Forced Sterilization: a Stain on California," Peter Irons, February 2003), from 1929, thirty states permitted forced human sterilizations. During this period of reproductive exploitation, 64,000 people were deemed mentally defective, morally and socially unfit, or too poor to keep their own children. They were sterilized through eugenics, selective human breeding, and social engineering programs.

California topped the list with 21,000 non-consensual sterilizations, Virginia came in second with approximately 8,000, and North Carolina was third with 7,600. *The Richmond Times-Dispatch* article stated, "The system granted excessive power to social workers, browbeat women into being sterilized and had ineffective safeguards..."

Carrie Buck, an 18-year-old unmarried mother, was the first person sterilized under Virginia's 1924 law. Ms. Buck, according to *The Los Angeles Times*, "was not mentally retarded or abnormal in any way but was sterilized because she had a child out of wedlock and was considered morally delinquent.'"

After further exploration into the history of adoption, it is interesting to discover that the cause of infertility for some married couples was a direct result of World War II – of men returning home from war to their wives with venereal diseases that rendered one or both incapable of having their own children. It is also interesting to note that some of the young girls who did not become pregnant (while other girls did), had their own inborn safety net – their as-yet-undiscovered infertility (rather than obeying the dictates of society by not having sex). Therefore, surrendering mothers' only "crime" was getting caught, and, for that crime, they were punished by the coerced removal of their babies by adoption and a life-long sentence of loss and grief.

Today, these mothers find themselves still in hiding,

searching, or agonizing through painful reunions (many of which end abruptly). They continue to struggle with issues directly relating to their surrender experience.

Many exiled mothers are offended by the term "triad" because it does not apply to them or their children. A triad has three equal sides. Adoption has only one side – the side of people who adopt. People who adopt are the only ones who win through adoption, the only ones who do not lose anything (their infertility was not lost because of adoption) and they are the ones who gain – (they get a baby). There is no three-way balance as suggested by the word "triad." Adoptees and their exiled mothers are the only ones who lose and they continue to lose considerably.

> "All the residents... were within weeks of deciding whether to keep or to part with their baby. Yet they had only the haziest notions of what either solution would mean in practical or emotional terms. In all but a few cases, they were ignorant of the most basic facts about adoption or the facilities they might find helpful if they kept the baby." – *Mother and Baby Homes, A Survey of Homes for Unmarried Mothers*, Jill Nicholson (1968)

Good Faith, Bad Faith

What did surrendering mothers know of legal matters when they were teenagers and young adults (especially before the advent of the Information Age)? Did they think to ask for a lawyer? No, most did not. Did they think to question the legality of the methods used by the social workers? Again, most did not. They blindly trusted in the adults who were "guiding" them through their pregnancies, through the baby warehouses (maternity facilities) while diverting their babies into the arms of the married and more financially-secure. These mothers were taught to respect elders and to respect authority. Why would these young women suspect that social workers would ever deceive them?

As they continue to question what occurred, mothers wonder whether they had legal rights and, if so, what they might have been, what they *should* have been.

> "Breach Of Duty: [...] any violation or omission of a legal or moral duty [...] the neglect or failure to fulfill in a just and proper manner the duties of an office or fiduciary employment."

> "Informed Consent: A person's agreement to allow something to happen that is based on a full disclosure of facts needed to make the decision intelligently." – *Black's Law Dictionary* – Centennial Edition (1891–1991)

Many now know that a lawyer should have been hired to oversee their legal interests, one *not* being paid by an adoption agency. It was a conflict of interests for social workers at adoption agencies to hire lawyers to draft adoption papers that surrendering mothers were asked, encouraged, or told to sign. Those lawyers were hired to protect the rights and interests of the adoption agencies and the people who were adopting. They were distinctly *not* hired to represent surrendering mothers or to protect their rights and interests (as no one represented the interests of the vulnerable young women).

In addition, many mothers are now beginning to recognize that many social workers did *not* perform their express duty of informing them about other means that might have allowed them to keep their baby. This included Aid to Families with Dependent Children (AFDC) assistance, the right to sue the father for child support, the right to place their baby temporarily in foster care until they were able to obtain jobs and/or a place to live, and the right to return for their baby within a legally-designated timeframe. In almost every case, these rights, these "choices," were not explained to surrendering mothers. This was bad faith and a breach of duty by social workers who were entrusted with this responsibility by society and as agents of state governments.

Many mothers were instructed by social workers, either immediately after giving birth (or at some point later), to sign adoption papers *without* a lawyer present. Many were not told to read the papers nor informed about what they contained, nor were they asked if they had questions. According to the American Bar Association Model Rules of Professional Conduct, Rule 4.3: Dealing With Unrepresented Persons: "The lawyer shall not give legal advice to an unrepresented person, other than the advice to secure counsel, if the lawyer knows or reasonably should know that the interests of such a person are or have a reasonable possibility of being in conflict with the interests of the client."

In this regard, it seems clear that the legal rights of surrendering mothers were completely ignored and severely abused.

> "Bad Faith: The opposite of good faith," generally implying or involving actual or constructive fraud, or a design to mislead or deceive another, or a neglect or refusal to fulfill some duty or some contractual obligation, not prompted by an honest mistake as to ones rights or duties, but by some interested or sinister motive. The term "bad faith" is not simply bad judgment or negligence, but rather it implies the conscious doing of a wrong because of a dishonest purpose or moral obliquity; it is different from the negative idea of negligence in that it contemplates a state of mind affirmatively operating with furtive design or ill will. An intentional tort which results from breach of duty imposed as consequence of relationship established by contract."
> – *Black's Law Dictionary* – Centennial Edition (1891–1991)

Persuasive Coercions

Brainwashing, thought reform, and coercive persuasion were psychological methods used often during times of war. Today these methods are most commonly used by cults, but they have also been used by societies to control and influence certain segments of the population for different reasons.

Coercion is an important aspect of a mother's institutional maternity experience that must be considered and explored. It should be clear about how the role of coercion heavily played on the surrender of babies to adoption. Six conditions, according to Drs. Margaret Thayer Singer and Richard Ofshe, psychologists and respected experts in thought reform, were present during the confinements by mothers in maternity facilities: (1) keep person unaware; (2) maintain control over their time and environment; (3) create a sense of powerlessness; (4) use rewards and punishments to inhibit behavior reflecting the person's former identity; (5) use rewards and punishments to promote the group's beliefs and behaviors; and (6) use logic and authority that permits no feedback.

> "Coercion: Compelled to compliance; constrained to obedience, or submission... Compelling by force... may be actual, direct... as where one party is constrained by subjugation to another to do what [her] free will would refuse..." – *Black's Law Dictionary* – Centennial Edition (1891–1991)

> "Conflict of Interest: Refers to a situation when someone, such as a lawyer or public official, has competing professional or personal obligations or personal or financial interests that would make it difficult to fulfill his duties fairly." – *The 'Lectric Law Library*

> "There is... a common theme... that runs through all legal definitions... of what constitutes coercion... It is the idea that in coercion the victims will is overthrown, or overcome, or overborne, or destroyed, or neutralized, or subverted... And that also... is at issue when there are allegations of coercive persuasion, or brainwashing, or thought reform. In some way, you overcome or destroy or subvert the will of the person... the will is not just overcome but is then also dominated by the person who is doing this. So that the victim then becomes a kind of agent, a tool, an extension of the will, of the coercer." – *Coercion, Coercive Persuasion, and the*

Law, Herbert Finagrett (1997)

Is this what happened to surrendering mothers? Were they manipulated, deceived, brainwashed, and/or coerced? Did the adoption industry, through social workers, overcome a mother's will by detaching her from her family (which removed all forms of support she might have had), break her will by assigning her a chore, by destroying her defenses (by stating she was unworthy to parent her child), and by making her feel as if choosing to parent would forever ruin her life and the life of her child? The answer is compelling.

With no options given, no place to live, and no help, the mother's experience of surrendering her baby was a gun-to-the-head situation. Mr. Finagrett continues: "The gun-at-the-head situation no doubt typically includes some kind of psychological turmoil or even mental trauma in the victim... getting at the meaning of coercion is saying that when there is coercion the victim has 'no real choice'...'no free choice'... 'no fair choice.'"

Many mothers who were expected to surrender were young and untested. In order to recognize motherhood, a woman must be allowed to experience it, however, they were denied this right. How could they have *fully* appreciated the depth of their loss at that time?

Mr. Finagrett, in his paper, goes on to say, "It seems to me that, on the whole, the more likely legal terrain for such claims [of coercion] would be defined by the claim that the purported victim had been rendered... incompetent in some respect or degree... In the end this is a factual question: How gross was the wrong done the victim, or how gross is the incompetence?"

Weren't surrendering mothers automatically ruled incompetent – mentally and physically incompetent – *in all ways incompetent*? They were never afforded the right to even *try* to raise their children. They should then ask, "How gross was the wrong done to them and their children?"

In all the world, in all of life, through God and nature, the most sacred bond is between a mother and her child. To lose that relationship, as in a mother losing her child to adoption, and a child losing her mother, is the most traumatic, the most "grossly wrong," the most grievous loss imaginable.

I have great sadness that I did not grow up with my own family. Much therapy and inner-child work led me to believe that the thing I must do is to help others heal their pain.

Joe Soll is a psychotherapist and lecturer and the author of *Adoption Healing: A Path to Recovery* and co-author of *Evil Exchange* and *Fatal Flight*. Since 1989, Mr. Soll has organized and coordinated ten international mental-health conferences on adoption. Mr. Soll has appeared on radio and television over 300 times, given over 150 lectures on adoption-related issues, and has been acknowledged, quoted, or featured in over four-dozen publications. He was portrayed as a therapist in an NBC made-for-television movie about adoption, played himself in the HBO Special *Reno Finds Her Mom*, was featured in the 2000 Global Japan award-winning documentary, *Adoption Therapist: Joe Soll*, and in the MediaStorm 2011 documentary, *Broken Lines*. He has also been profiled by The International Museum of Women.

On Behalf of Scottish Mothers

IN 1963, I THOUGHT the world was my oyster. I was about to leave school and walk into full-time employment, courtesy of my beloved cousin, who was manageress of a business. Believe me, jobs were extremely rare in the small seaside town of Stranraer, in Dumfries, and in Galloway, where I lived then. I was introduced to the company accountant (my son's future father) who explained the mundane details of taxes and national insurance contributions (which I protested at a little). Being so green in the work place, and working the long hours for £2 pounds 10/-shillings imperial, I grumbled a little. The money belonged to me, I worked for it. I truly was the greenest-as-green when it came to forming relationships with the opposite sex at that time. I never realized that I was being woo'd by my son's future father. The last thing on my mind was love, but rather I was full of independence, wanting to save for all sorts of adventures, and buying my own clothes were real priorities (as hand-me-downs were a country-wide practice).

After about five or six months, I finally went out on my first date. I challenge anybody to tell me that falling in love for the first time in life is not the most wonderful experience. Yes, the world was beautiful from behind my rose-tinted glasses.

In 1966, I found myself pregnant on a train, leaving Scotland for this country they call "England" (that I only knew through geography at school) – banished, broken, terrified – all because I fell in love with the wrong man in the wrong era. He was the wrong colour and religion, but I just saw him as this lovely person I had fallen in love with.

I had to don the mantle of *fugitive* for my sins.

The mother and baby home is far enough away from home that the only means of contact is by letter.

In my mind, I conjured up "caring Christians" as it was a Salvation Army Home, called *Hopedene*, that I was heading for in Newcastle-upon-Tyne.

"Austere" would have been an understatement and I was continually in a state of high-anxiety. I was never greeted with kindness. Indeed if I had been, I would have needed resuscitation if I ever heard, "How are you today, Marion? And how is *your baby*?" Instead (more times than I care to remember) I heard, "Are your chores complete? Where are you next working, girl?"

The bedrooms in the attic were freezing and you got one bath per week. The rest of the time, we all topped and tailed in a communal wash room. No pre-natal care or instruction, *absolutely nothing*, and the food was atrocious. We never received fresh fruit. Vegetables consisted of a spoonful of cabbage or a spoonful of carrot, once or twice a week *only*. The rest was not fit for human consumption.

Like soldiers, we were marched to the Salvation Army temple every Sunday and made to sit in the penitence forms (where the whole congregation could see us). We would often hear whispers like, "That poor baby, it does not know what is coming to it" and "She looks as if she could drop that baby right now." Yes, we were the goldfish in the bowl.

I had the full onslaught of labor, but not a single painkiller, "you suffer for your sin." By suffering the whole labour without medication, I was screamed at for falling off the bed when told not to, then caught again and slapped hard for not doing as I was told. Made to wipe up the mess I had created when the enema decided to evacuate at the bedside instead of the loo. Yes, nearing delivery, yet wiping up my own mess, when the witch from Endor was out of the room.

The two officers at my delivery were, as I believed, qualified midwives, yet I never received proper aftercare. We only learned from each other (bearing in mind that we never got sex education at school and there were *no* pre-natal classes preparing us for motherhood).

Because of their negligence, I have attended gynecologists and urologists, from 1967 to this very day, with a number of unsuccessful operations, treatments, and medications, to no avail. Topping it all, when we young mothers attended the local hospital for injections, we were separated from the ordinary patients. I was always referred to as "the Scotch girl with the half-caste." This treatment is indelible. It is there continually in my flashbacks, in my dreams, a never ending abyss of fear and sorrow.

My beautiful baby son was born at 9 P.M., but he was taken from me immediately and I was told that I could not see him till tomorrow. I was not even allowed to touch or hold him. It was the longest darkest night of pinning and pain, yet in my soul, I wanted to tell the world I had this beautiful baby. I remember hoping his dad would come and rescue us from this nightmare. I was trapped in a hellhole of a place with no means of escape.

I was removed to a ward for new mums where my hell truly began. I have inverted nipples, and there was no way my son could feed. One mum did everything in her power to log him onto my breast, resulting in cracked areola. I was in agony. After a week, I was fed a horrendous amount of a drug, named Stilboestrol (sixteen pills per day), to dry up my milk in order to start bottle feeding. I became very sick, but you could not be sick, because there was no one to care for you. Because of my weak state and my lack of milk, my baby lost weight. The evil woman threatened me with exposure to the media, as she insisted that I was deliberately trying to starve my son. I was just so unwell.

Babies from one-week-old were fed a teaspoonful of custard or semolina at night to fatten them up for adoption.

Life continued in this vein, incarceration under a penal-servitude regime. My son was three months old when I was told they had adopters for him and he would be going soon. That struck such fear in me, I just could not believe it. Then some days later, I was told that they would not be taking my son, as they wanted a perfect baby, and had noticed that he had an eye defect. (Is there any greater cruelty than this evil exchange they call "adoption"?)

As my baby was getting older, policy only allowed me to be with him at feeding time. The rest of the time he was under the care of staff, yet I often heard him crying. He was separated from the newborns and set in a room entirely on his own with absolutely no stimulation. It was dark drab grey, with the most awful cot and high chair, torn bed sheets and blankets, similar to what was in his pram for when he was put outside. He had no toys, so I started to knit some, and I knitted three pram sets for him with matinee-coats, boots, mitts, and hats. I did extra chores for the girls and they paid me little so I bought wool. During my year incarcerated, I received one letter from my father, but nothing from my mother.

Breaking the rules brought heavy punishment, and I broke them often by sneaking into my baby's room to cuddle and play with him. I had warnings. When I heard the footsteps coming, I would hide under his cot, but didn't realize my feet were protruding. "Banishment to the Doss House for you, girl!" And so I was sent to a facility called North Ashfield. *How can I forget that?* "You will leave after eight o'clock every night, and you will be up in the nursery for six in the morning, and you will be there 'till adoption takes place."

"Well, girl, you will be glad to know we are having a

Christmas fare. There will be potential adopters coming to buy at the fare. So for the few days and nights while it takes place, you will take your working clothes off. You dress yourself and the baby nicely and look smart."

I was dressed nicely and my son was dressed like a Christmas turkey for the shoppers. *Hey, bingo!* My son's adopters saw us, made inquiries, and got the ball rolling. They had a teenaged daughter (who came and saw him) and I was told that she wanted him for Christmas, but it was explained to her that there were procedures. Meantime, she could name "*our new baby*," which she did: "Christopher" (for he was got for Christmas) and "Andrew," because his soon-to-be-obsolete mother was Scottish. How that impacted, seared, affected my whole life. I bloody despise Christmas with a perfect hatred, because when I read the *Bible*, true Christianity shines forth, but I never once experienced biblical Christianity the whole time I was at the mother and baby home.

Since learning that Pope Gregory IV (394 A.D.) chose Christ's birthday to be on the 25th December (marrying up with all the Pagan festivals (Saturnalia) in Rome at that time), it gives me leverage to show the parallels with Christmas and adoption. *The great big lie. Bearing false witness.* That's what adoption is. My son has a false name and a false history. As does the Lord Jesus Christ according to present-day Hebrew history. They believe that Jesus was born in either late September or in early October.

Most people living in the central belt of Scotland and the lowlands are reared in our Bard's history and poetry. (The Bard, in this case, being "Rabbie Burns.")

"Your baby will be taken for adoption on Wednesday, 25th January," on Burn Supper Day. How could I ever forget his adoption day?

Wee Ode to My Son:

"Till awe the seas gang dry,
and the rocks melt way the sun,

you'll always be my precious wee lamb,
and I will always be your mum."

These are cold and calculated words: "Now, no tears. You are the luckiest girl. Your baby is going to a family that has businesses. He will never want. He will have a real mum and dad to care for him. And he has a teenage sister to spoil him. You are so lucky, girl! Now go and do your chores with a glad heart."

I can tell you, to this day, these words ringing in my ears at that time. I had a physical pain in my chest and, instantly, I had a sickness. I could not eat. They noticed this and had me shadowed, but even tea was hard to keep down.

I was ushered into a room, far away from the main area (so no one could see or hear) and given a new layette to put on my son. "Please let me put these beautiful knitted clothes on him," she said. I had offered my pram set for him and a lovely cardigan. "Don't be silly. His parents will want him in these *bought* clothes," the evil woman said.

To my wee lamb, "I will love you till awe the seas gang dry, and the rocks melt wae the sun, mummy loves you."

I was dying on my feet. I shook uncontrollably. My beautiful baby was anxious. "What's up, mummy?" This is what his wee face said to me. "Please mummy, don't cry." *Oh God, please God, help me. I can't go through with this. My baby is nine-months-old. He is my life. Please come and get me, Hussain! Our baby needs us.* I picked up those leather shoes they brought for him and dropped to my knees. The shoes were made in my home town. *Baby Deer Shoes, Stranraer, Scotland.*

My strength was gone, but an angel appeared in the form of an officer. She was from Bonnie Briggs, near Edinburgh, and like me, a real Christian. She weeps with me. She sees my baby crying. She held me and we wept together. I still could not eat. "You need sustenance, girl. Here, tea and a biscuit."

"I don't want tea and a biscuit," *I want my baby.*

I could not sleep, was shadowed for the next week, and then told that I could go home after another week (time enough to make sure the adopters were happy with *my* baby). *How bloody cruel is that?* It was their policy to keep me busy for that week and then, they assumed, I would never think about recent events ever again. To them, we were only teenage girls with no feelings and no soul. They thought that we would get over our babies being taken from us and that we would get on with life, just at the drop of a hat, as if we were programmed automatons.

I had to wash walls, and paint the officer's quarters, and all the while, I could hear my baby cry. I knew all his little idiosyncrasies. I could feel him, smell him and, throughout the years of separation, my nightmare was always the same: my baby standing up in the cot, his arms outstretched for me to pick him up but, when I reach for him, he disappears. They are as vivid today as they were 44 years ago.

Scotland and the U.K. were heartless places for unmarried mothers forty-four years ago. The so-called Church failed us miserably, yet they made a great profit from selling our babies. When I look at the story of David and Bathsheba and read other passages, like "I will heal your broken heart, and bind up your wounded soul" (Psalm 147, Verse 3), I see what true forgiveness, what real caring, is.

I returned home and was told by my mother, "Don't unpack your suitcase, you will be off in a day or so. You can never live at home again. You make your own way in life now. Go as far away from here as possible. You will take this secret to the grave. You may never tell a living soul about this."

I was beyond feeling, beyond pain. Death would have been such a comfort. My father walked with me to the bus station to board the first bus to Glasgow. I arrived less than five hours later. I ended up in a women's hostel. *Was this really happening? All this punishment because I fell in love? How could this be? How could no one help me and my baby? Where were our legal rights? Where were our welfare rights? Where were our human rights?* Never once did I see a solicitor who could tell me what my entitlements were.

Adoption, to me, is the cruelest transaction in the history of the human race and it should be banished to the annals of history.

Suicidal and sacked from my first two jobs in Glasgow (for crying at work), I locked myself away in my room at the hostel. I attended the doctors for stomach pains. He told me I was wound up like a corkscrew and gave me antidepressants. I suffered all my life with ulcers and now have a cluster of polyps, severe IBS, and nervous anxiety. I became anorexic and lost quite a bit of weight, but was brought back from that dark abyss. Mogadon and Valium have become the friends that help me make it through another day.

The doctors don't want to know. For mothers of loss to adoption, post-traumatic stress disorder is forever. But in Scotland, there is no help for mothers (unless you pay to see a private physician).

I live daily with bereavement. The loss is truly a bottomless abyss of sorrow.

Marion McMillan has worked as a volunteer in childrens' homes, as a foster parent, and as a registered nursery nurse. She has fifteen years in the field as a learning facilitator supporting families in crisis, mostly single mums. Marion is pro-active in campaigning for justice for the "Forgotten Mothers," founding a local support group, "Podanoit," for families separated by adoption and lobbying The Scottish Adoption Policy Review Board at every opportunity. In 2005, Marion spoke to The Scottish Parliament, which led to participation in a televised documentary, and to three articles in national newspapers. At the inauguration of the Scottish Christian Party (SCP) at St. Andrew's, she was invited to speak on the subject of adoption history and trauma. Marion represented the SCP West of Scotland as a candidate in regional elections, campaigning on adoption issues by pointing out the neglect and injustice suffered by its victims and survivors.

My Inner Heart:
From an Illiterate Birthmother

MY NAME IS LAKSHMI and I lost two daughters to intercountry adoption. I am the wife to Malkaiah in Jogipet village. Jogipet is in the Medak District, located in the state of Andrah Pradesh within India. I've given birth to two babies and named them Manjula, "lovely and charming," and Bhagya, "fortune and faith."

While Manjula and Bhagya were growing up in my care and protection, a lady by the name of Fatima, a sari village vendor, regularly visited my house and saw my girls. Fatima and I became friends because of her frequent visits.

One day, Fatima asked me to keep my daughters in a hostel at Gandhi Nagar in Hyderabad, near the Jublie Bus Station. My mind was full of thoughts and uneasy feelings while Fatima asked me to let my girls go with her to the hostel. My facial expressions showed that I was not willing and doubtful.

Fatima continued to explain to me that I was an illiterate

mother who lived in a rural area that provided no educational facilities. I questioned Fatima. "Will my daughters come and go regularly to the festivals and holidays?" Fatima's answered, "Oh, yes! Why not? They will come and go. I will make them keep in touch with you, also."

After much discussion, I relented and accepted Fatima's explanation for taking my daughters. I was satisfied that my children would have the opportunity to get an education, especially since I was unable to get one.

I signed a piece of white paper for my daughters to be taken away from me and placed in the hostel as Fatima had suggested. However, I didn't understand the document I was signing. I did not understand that I would not have the ability to see my daughters again. Fatima took my daughters and left. I thought I would see them again.

Six months later, my daughters had not been returned home, as Fatima had promised. She had told me that Manjula and Bhagya would come-and-go frequently, but my daughters had never been back home. I cried and begged for Fatima to bring my daughters to me, but she was unresponsive to my pleas.

Eventually, the girls' father had had enough. He was very angry at me. He yelled, "Why did you do this?" He was angry at Fatima, which motivated Fatima to have us visit the hostel in Gandhinagar to finally see our children.

When we reached the hostel, Fatima showed us our daughters from behind the glass walls where our daughters couldn't see us, but we could see them. I was so happy to see my daughters. They looked good, happy, grown up, and even appeared chubby! Malkaiah and I went home satisfied.

After a year, my husband and I again traveled to the hostel, but our daughters were not there! When we asked the hostel warden about our children, we were told that they had been sent to Vikarabad. And later, we learned, our daughters had been sold to people in the United States.

The Reunion

After five years, my beautiful daughter, Manjula, finally came to Jogipet with her adoptive father. I was so emotional and distraught, I cried nonstop. My daughter cried along with me.

For three days they came and went, staying in Hyderabad, the capital of Andhra Pradesh – 83 kilometers away, at night. I asked the adoptive father to allow for me to keep my daughter to stay with me for at least one night, but he rejected my request. I was surprised that Manjula just stood by and listened to the adoptive father. If he told her to eat, she ate. Whatever he instructed her to do, she obeyed. At first, I was surprised by her behavior. Then I became upset and angry when I realized that there was nothing I could do.

The adoptive father said that my younger daughter, Bhagya, was not ready to see me. Therefore, she did not come with Manjula on this trip. Instead, I must wait until he told me that she was ready, which would be after her 18th birthday.

The day my daughter left, I cried so much and caught hold of the adoptive father's legs in an attempt to keep Manjula with me or to, otherwise, take me to his place to stay with my daughters. He replied, "By coming with us, what will you do there? Will you be my watchdog?" These were the words that this man said to me.

I was fighting, crying, and demanding my daughters' freedom. One visit was not enough for me. It was not enough for me. Reunion was a happy event, but daughters should be in touch with their parents regularly.

No mother should experience this kind of trauma. This trauma should not happen to any mother. I can't release my inner turmoil, which I have been carrying since my daughters had been taken away from me. It's so horrible, pathetic, totally unfair, and unjust.

Update: Early in 2013, Arun Dohle of Against Child Trafficking and Anjali Pawar of Sakhee Child's Rights collected Indian families (of adoption loss) from the rural countryside and helped them into the city during an Adoption Conference. Usually, during these types of conferences, adopted people and their adoptive parents (along with adoption professionals and experts) are the only guests invited to attend. This was a momentous event because for the first time in the history of the industry, families were taken to the conference site, hoping to state their losses and be heard inside the New Delhi Hotel.

Waiting to be acknowledged, the family members wore white paper bibs, expressing their concerns: "Lost my child to adoption," "I am missing my daughter," "We are searching for my child," "I am a victim of adoption trafficking," and "Where is my sister?"

Devastatingly, these families, including **Lakshmi**, were refused entrance to the venue and, in fact, were not even allowed to attend any of the sessions. Rather, they were permitted downstairs in a holding room near the hotel and then told to wait outside.

These Indian families continue on with their lives, still upset, with little hope to ever be reunited. They are grateful, at least, for the little public attention they received during that attempt and the rare opportunity to attend an adoption conference.

Families around the world hope that the Western fervor to adopt "orphans," which perpetuates the global demand for children, will eventually be stopped.

Lakshmi still waits to have regular communication with her two grown daughters.

– **The Vance Twins**

Fatherhood Stolen

An Interview with an Australian Father of Adoption Loss:

Interviewer: So, Cameron. Just, if you can, takes us through who you were when your girlfriend got pregnant. And what your time was like together and how that changed once that happened.

Cameron: Well, we were late teenagers. We started going out together when she was in year eleven [in high school]. Most of our time together was when she was in year twelve and a bit beyond that. I met her through sport – I was at university for the time that we were together and she was at school.

So we were fairly typical northern-beaches late teenagers, just hanging around the beach. [A] fairly carefree time. I worked at a squash centre at Chatswood. And, even at that young age, we made plans about what our future was going to be. We were pretty tight, yeah. There was no, sort of, question that we hadn't found our life's partner. We were pretty convinced that we had.

Interviewer: And then what happened?

Cameron: Well, obviously, I didn't know, but just after she finished her HSC [High School Certificate], I found out that she was pregnant. She must have known, but we hadn't seen each other for a while – while she was doing the HSC.

And so, to cut a very long convoluted story short, when her parents found out, they went absolutely ballistic. Her father chased me around the house with a knife in his hand. And he beat her up in the kitchen one day while I was there, that sort of behaviour. And I was getting reports from her of what was going on in the house. And he basically – the family – decided, basically, to lock her in her room for the last three months of her pregnancy to try and keep her away from me.

I, actually, at one stage, asked the social worker a direct question. I said, "How do I stop this adoption?" And she said, "You can't." Which I now know is completely untrue. But you're relying on people who you think are professionals and who you think have the knowledge.

I went to the chamber magistrate at Manly Court to try and see if he had any angle on this. I was caught between spending money on lawyers, which I didn't have, because I was a uni[versity] student, and trying to spend what little money I had setting up a baby room at home, and trying to make some sort of provision for bringing a child home.

So, that's who we were, and that's how we were thinking at the time.

Interviewer: And your key issue is that you feel that you were completely shut out of the process. As the biological father, you were removed?

Cameron: Yeah, well, I now know it was standard practice.

But yeah, completely shut out of Ellen's[1] life. Shut out of my girlfriend's life by her being locked in this house. And it wasn't until 18 years later, when I started getting some papers, that I discovered that the agency knew all this stuff.

They knew that there was physical abuse going on in the house. They describe certain things in some of the papers. They knew. My name is all over the paperwork, so they knew about me. They knew I was making noises that I didn't want this to happen. I didn't want my offspring to be disappearing somewhere else. But I was given this blank sort of, "There's no way you can stop it. Only Ellen and her family can make this decision." Which, at the time, seemed a bit strange, but my father had just gone through a divorce and I saw how he had been treated through the courts and I thought, "Well, maybe that's just how things happen."

Then when our child was born and I actually turned up at the hospital, and there was about probably six-to-ten days when, I think, there was hospitalisation there.

So, I was in-and-out of the hospital and, a couple of times, I turned up when the consent taker was sitting there with the papers and all that. And I stopped that process happening. But there were situations where Ellen's father was coming into the hospital, and slapping her around in the hospital, and no-one came to help her. You know? So, as far as my involvement, I was trying to get involved, you know? I should be part of this process. My DNA is all over the paperwork that exist and, yet, I still lost my daughter to adoption.

And, interestingly, I heard from women who lost children recently, that they were being interrogated about this in another forum, and the question was said (or the statement was said), "Well, you signed an adoption consent. So, you know, that's the end of it." Well, they can't say that to me. I didn't sign anything. I was very adamant. In fact, I was asked to sign and I just looked at the consent taker, like... In fact, I distinctly

---

[1] Ellen is not the real name of the person involved.

remember, in the hospital, when all those papers were spread all over my girlfriend's bed, I just looked at her, and I said, "This is wrong. This is completely wrong." And all the paperwork was folded up and taken away.

So that was my attitude. And yet, I didn't sign anything and to this day, I do not agree. A relative of mine recently said to me – I asked her, "What was your perception of my attitude back then?" And she said, "Cam, you were so determined not to lose your child." And yet, here we are having this conversation. I did lose my child. And it's like, you know, I now know there were all sorts of clauses in all sorts of acts that I could have invoked if someone had just… Hadn't been so convinced that they were going to take my child.

Interviewer: So, just make it clear for us. What were your intentions once you found out your girlfriend was pregnant?

Cameron: Our intentions were always to get married. And then, when we found out she was pregnant, it was just a matter of, "Oh, well," we'll have to bring that forward. And so, even in fact, the first day in the hospital, we were discussing this, and she leaned forward to me, and her mother was in the room, and [Ellen] leaned forward to me and she said, "Cam I want this little girl to be Rebecca Horn." And I said, "Yeah. So do I." I said, "Don't worry. We'll do it somehow."

But, by that time, there was so much pressure. And I said, "Don't worry about it. We'll do it somehow. We'll do this." And we were, sort of, sitting knee-to-knee, on chairs, and our heads were touching. You know. And we were saying this – in front of her mother. And her mother was just having a conniption. She was having some sort of breakdown on one side of the room. But that was what we were discussing even in the hospital. There was never any other thought in our minds. It's still a mystery to me how they got her to sign those consent papers at a time when I wasn't there.

And then, when I met her again (about six weeks later), they took her back home, and they locked her up again. And once the revocation period was over, they basically put their foot in her back and said, "There you are. There's the world. Go out and get it."

So, she came back to my place one time and completely fell to pieces. She ended up in the fetal position under the table. I had to chase her around the house to stop her hurting herself. That's the sort of state of mind she was in at the end of all this.

And just on the marriage situation, in my papers, when I got my papers 18 years later, the adoption consent taker had made a note: "Cameron wanted to keep the baby, but marriage was not considered." Now, you know. That first part of that statement is absolutely true. Yes, "Cameron wanted to keep the baby" and Cameron wanted to keep Ellen, as well. You know?

And this, "Marriage was not considered." Well, I think, that's obviously her parents have insisted that be put down or it's just some piece of fantasy that the adoption agency has written there. Because our intention was always to get married.

Interviewer: What is clear is that they've admitted your intention was to keep the baby.

Cameron: Yeah.

Interviewer: But you were never given a look in.

Cameron: That's right. Well, I was never given any of the rights or responsibilities that were enshrined in law for fathers in 1980.

Interviewer: Your experience is not that common, though. I know you say there are others out there but, for most men, they seem to move on from this more easily than women can.

Cameron: Well, obviously, there's that physical connection for women. They carry the baby. They give birth to the baby. And then they physically have the baby taken off them at some stage. Someone reaches into their hands and takes it away. And all those sorts of things don't necessarily happen for the man. But, certainly right through, or from the period, those couple of months there, I was talking to my baby through the womb, and all those sorts of things, there was that same bond. And then of course, when she was born, I mean, I can still remember turning the corner and walking into that room and then there's the love of my life holding my child. You don't forget those sorts of things. I mean they talk about... People say about the adoptive parents, "Oh well, they're the ones that changed the pooey nappy." I was one of the first people to change a pooey nappy for my daughter. I held her, I mean, this was 1980. I mean, even as Ellen was giving birth, she said to me later (and, in fact, her mother confirmed this) while she was giving birth, she was saying, "Get Cam here. Someone get Cam here. Someone call Cam." And no one bothered to call. None of the nurses. And she was pleading with her mother, "Go and call Cam."

Well, as I say, I'm named right through all the paperwork. I know that Ellen put my name on all the registration forms. She put my name on all the paperwork. My name's everywhere. And yet, somewhere between all that paperwork being filled out, and someone at Births, Deaths, and Marriages deciding what they're going to put on a birth registration, my name gets removed. Now, do you want me to go into how I found out about this?

Interviewer: Yeah, sure.

Cameron: OK, well then 16 years later, the Information Act gets changed, and I just happened to be at work and a FAX came through to the wrong department. It was supposed to go to "News," but it came to me. And I looked at this, and I discovered that my daughter could go and get her original birth certificate at the age 16 and get certain information. So, I thought, *I better go check*, you know, that I'm there, because I didn't want her going to the address that was on the birth certificate because that was going to be the violent grandparents. And you don't know what sort of reception she's going to get there.

And I wanted her to come to me. I wanted her to find me, so I go and find out that I'm not named on the birth certificate. Then I have to go through this horrendous process, paying money and getting stat docs from Ellen and having to contact her husband. And disrupting her family and her life to put this right. And she had no hesitation in doing it. And they make you pay money, as well.

...removing the father, or making it appear that the father had disappeared, removes all responsibility from these adoption workers. All the responsibilities they have towards the father to basically get his consent. To ask to give him an opportunity to be involved in the process, to be involved in the child's life and future. And every time (that I've found, anyway) in the legal courts, where a father has challenged this (and there's four or five particular cases), every time that I've found where they've challenged this, the father's won. And so I think, *not having the father on the birth certificate, gives this illusion that neither of the parties knew.* The mother didn't know who the father was, either. I mean, it's ridiculous – thousands and thousands and thousands of birth certificates.

"30 Days"

Interviewer: So, we know you tried to stop it, but you did find out. And how did you react then?

Cameron: I actually can't remember how I found out. I think I just got a phone call at work saying, "She signed the papers." Something like that. "Your 30 days starts now." That was from either a friend of hers or from a member of the family. I actually, can't actually remember how I found out. But then as soon as I found out, I went 'round to her house. And I found all the windows in her room had been boarded up and nailed shut, and all that sort of stuff. So I couldn't get to her the way I had been previously, with the letters. So, I basically went home and waited out the 30 days, hoping I'd get a phone call.

Actually, I went home and I tried to phone her and every time the phone would get picked up by her mother. And the phone was right outside Ellen's room, so obviously she was being stopped from using the phone.

Anyway, after the 30 days, you know, I was watching the 30 days like you watch the clock sort-of-thing. And the 30 days came-and-went. And I remember that morning pretty clearly. That was just like (long pause) I don't even think I got out of bed. I just sort... she's gone.

Interviewer: So you were very aware of when that 30 days ended?

Cameron: Oh, yeah. Yeah. Yeah. I think I had it marked in my diary. I had every day marked in my diary. And, yeah. That 30 days came-and-went and I'd been told I couldn't intervene or couldn't make any change. And then, a couple of days after the 30 days, I got a phone call from Ellen saying that she was working just around the corner from my place. And I said to her, "Do you want me to come up there for lunch?" And she said, "No, you can't be seen in public with me." You know, she had gone to this, sort of, headspace.

She comes down to the house. We have lunch. I think we just stood in the hallway just holding each other for an hour. And then it was time to go and then a car went passed the house. And she just went absolutely berserk, saying, "It's dad. It's dad. He's come to get me. He's going to come in and kill me." He's going to do this. He's going to do that. And I said, "It's not your father." And I was chasing her around the house. She was trying to find somewhere to hide. I was chasing her around the house and, in the end, I had to wrestle her to the ground, and say to her, "Look, there's no one coming in. The car's gone. No one's bashing on the door. Nothing's happening." And she crawled underneath the table and just curled up in fetal position, crying. And so, I got under the table with her and just held her. And then, just like that, just like...

she just stopped and said, "I gotta go back to work." And just, basically, stood up, and she said, "Go outside and check there's nobody there." So I went outside and then saw she was sprinting back to work, which was probably 400 metres. And this was a girl who had just gone through this trauma.

And I also discovered (it was about another six weeks) she was still heavily bleeding. Which I now know, now I've had other kids, I now know that's not normal. So obviously there's some.... All this disintegration of this beautiful person that I was in love with.

We started trying to get our relationship going again and then, eventually, I got a letter from her one day, saying that she told her parents that we were still going out together. And they said to her right there and then, "You've got to choose either him or us." And I can quote it word-for-word, you know, from 32 years ago. She said, "With all that's happened I couldn't stand to lose my family, as well." And she said to me, "You'll get over this in time." And things like that.

But I still continued to see her for the next couple of years. Actually, she was working at a bank and [I] stood in line and went to her counter at the bank and she just...

We continued to see each other just for lunches and things over the next couple of years.

Interviewer: In the end, how did consent come to be signed?

Cameron: Well, to be honest with you, I actually don't know. I was trying to juggle work and going into the hospital to support my girlfriend and my child. And sometimes I'd be in there twice-a-day. And there were occasions where I had shifts and I was trying to work so I would have resources to bring a child home. I thought I was bringing a child home. So, there was a few days that I missed. On odd occasions, I went in there and they were in the process of signing an adoption consent.

One time when I went in, I intervened [o]n one of those occasions, I said, "Ellen what are you doing?" And I picked up the forms and I said, "This is an adoption consent form. Do you understand what you're doing?" And she said, "Yes. This will give me 30 more days to make the decision." And that's how it was being sold to her. And she said, "With all that's going on with my family, and all the pressure I, kind of, need this breathing space." And with all the pressure that was being put on her. So there were aspects like that [in] the sales pitch.

And, also, the people working in the hospital. There was no alternative being offered. And, consequently, on a day when I wasn't able to get in there, they [were] able to convince her to sign this consent. Now I know one of the arguments they put to her was that this will give you 30 extra days to make up this decision. And that looked very attractive because she was under such pressure – 30 days breathing space. But, you know, it was an adoption consent she was signing. And then when I saw her 30 days later, she was a basket case. And so was I. I counted down those 30 days. I mean, I got a phone call, I think, from a family friend saying that she'd signed the papers and that she was no longer at the hospital, "so don't bother coming." That's all I knew. I don't, to this day, I really don't know how she put pen to paper. And, in fact, I've seen the adoption consent. It's not even her correct name that's on there. So, you know, I can't really answer that question definitively.

The Word "Agency"

Cameron: But I went back to uni[versity] in 1981, after all this happened, and I was just a basket case. You know and I…. I had been going alright at uni until 1980. Then this happened. Went back to uni in 1981, and just, you know. I'll show you my transcript, it's just: fail, fail, fail. So I changed university, and I went, I thought, "I'll do P.E. I'll do teaching P.E." So, I had to do anatomy and I had to [learn] all this biology and anatomy. And come the end of my biology class, I'd passed everything, I was doing okay. And our final report for biology was the human reproductive system. And, you know, we had all term to do this, and I was repeatedly going down to the library. I'd open the books (back in the days of book), open the books and look at all these diagrams and babies. And I just thought I was being lazy. I just thought I'm just being, you know. I blamed myself. But I'd just blank out for hours. I'd sit in the library with all these books open, thinking, "I've got to do this assignment." You know. "You've got to do this assignment to pass." I'd passed the exam. I'd passed all my other assignments. This was the big forty-percenter at the end. And I just couldn't do it. I couldn't physically bring myself to put pen-to-paper and actually do this, looking at all these diagrams. And I couldn't figure out why. And, in the end, one of my lecturers got hold of me and said, "Look, you've passed everything." And I still didn't know. I just said to him, "Oh, look, just fail me." I didn't care. And he said, "Look, just give me a piece of paper with your name written on it. And the title of the thing. You've passed everything. You've passed without this. Give me something I can put an 'F' on it. And you'll at least pass this module.

Years later, like 18 years later, when I'm going through reunion, I suddenly realised this is why I was blacking out. Two years later I'm blacking out looking at reproductive, you know, babies coming through reproductive channels. You know, diagrams of the human reproductive system. I'd be there for hours, just blank. And it was the trauma. I now realise it was the trauma from what had happened having my child taken away. I just couldn't go through that process. And, even now, I still have certain words I find I hesitate on. Most of them, funnily enough, start with "A." But one word in particular that I have a real problem with is the word "agency." I can say it now because I've really concentrated to say it. But I only discovered this when I started lecturing in advertising. Obviously, that word comes up all the time. And I'd be standing up in front of the class, and I couldn't say that word. And, I'd just come to a complete mental blank. So obviously, there's some psychological impasse in my mind, with words like "agency." I mean, I find the word "adoption" pretty traumatic, as well, but I've just had to train myself to say that word over and over.

Interviewer: The consent form did get signed...

Cameron: Yeah...

Interviewer: ...by the mother. How did that happen if you were still so against it?

Cameron: Well, I don't really know. I know I went in there—I was going in the hospital reasonably regularly and, when I say that, on odd occasions, it was twice a day. On other occasions there'd be a day between where I'd miss it. And that was because I was actually continuing to work, trying to make some money, so I could, at least, put together something to support the child I thought I was going to be bringing home. So, on a couple of occasions, I missed days being there because I had shifts at the sports centre where I was working. And probably (hindsight's a wonderful thing), I shouldn't have been working, because I wasn't working very efficiently, either. But on one of these occasions, I don't know how this adoption consent got signed. I've seen it. And I've seen her name on it. And, in fact, she hasn't signed her real name, either. But somehow, they've got in there on a day that I wasn't there. Her parents, obviously, I know her father went in there and was physically abusing her and sitting on top of her in the bed and smacking her around and all this sort of stuff. That happened on other occasions. Other people witnessed that. So, I assume this [type] of pressure came upon her at a time that I wasn't there. And I just got a terse phone call. You know, a day or two later. So I knew, I kind of knew, she was no longer at the hospital. But to this day, I don't know how that adoption consent form got signed. I've never been able to – in fact, I said to her, when we met up again, I said to Ellen, "How did you sign? How did you come to sign this thing?" And she said, she just basically said she was all alone and isolated, and this sort of thing, and even I wasn't there. She just kept saying, "Oh, well, where was I?" So the fact that I wasn't there for a day, they've been able to use that. I don't know what was said, but the best that I could get out of her was that when I was needed to stop this thing yet again, I wasn't there on a particular occasion. That's the best that I can come up with for that event, because it's a mystery to me, to this day, how she came to sign that thing.

Reunion

Interviewer: I think it's fair to say that you're quite obsessed with this issue. You'd probably deny that.

Cameron: I do have other parts to my life.

Interviewer: When you had the reunion with your daughter, did that give you any sense of closure? Did that answer some questions? Has it been better since then?

Cameron: No, it's been much worse. And, in fact, the grief and the... because now you can actually see the result. And as far as I'm concerned, the result is not that pleasing.

Interviewer: Just take it back then. Tell us about the reunion and what happened there.

Cameron: Well, this is not something that gets better over time. Because as you get older, as you live, you learn more and more about what's been taken away from you. And so you learn more and more about the enormity of what's been stolen.

So, at first, it's this thing that's happened. And it has been horrendous. It's been this terrible, sort of, trauma and it's been this event. But then as you see babies and you think, *Oh, that's cute. Where's mine?* You see. You watch other people, you watch little people growing up, and then you have kids of your own. Kids you're allowed to keep! And so you learn a whole other aspect of what's been stolen from you.

Then, as you were saying, you meet your offspring that's been taken and she's.... You can tell she's been hurt by this event. You can tell that, despite every effort that's been done on the part of her adoptive parents, there's still tragedy, and there's still pain, and there's still anger and hurt, and there's still all this stuff that's in her that's derived from her removal from, particularly, her mother, but removal from her parents, her biological story. And so, somehow, she's got to cope with that. And so, you see all this coping. You see a lot of pain. And then, it's been 14 years since I first met her – and some of the response that I've had (or lack of response). I mean, even when someone is not responding to you, they're still communicating to you. And so, you see more pain, and more anger, and more hurt, and more judgment. And I don't know if you can hate your biological kin without hating yourself to some extent.

So, there's all these issues, that are imprinted upon this person who's otherwise might have had a very different life. And [there] certainly wouldn't have been the money floating around that there has been in her life, but that's another thing. I see this complete reliance on materialism and emotional and soulful sorts of things don't seem to matter. Only the material matters. Well, that's only half-a-human being, as far as I'm concerned, walking around. I'm sort of getting a bit existential here, but you know that's what I see.

Interviewer: Well, just tell us how the reunion came about. But what your expectations were and how it felt on that day (and afterwards).

Cameron: I think two people coming into a reunion have a lot of fantasy and a lot of unreal expectations. And I think, also, there's no textbook, particularly for father-daughter reunions. And so they're fraught with all sorts of minefields. And really, my daughter and I stepped on every single one of them. And I've since spoken to a lot of men and I've been able to say, "Look, avoid this and avoid that," and they've had much more successful reunions.

Our reunion was, as far as I'm concerned, a complete disaster. We met down under the Sydney Harbour Bridge. That was the first time I'd ever seen her. She had actually seen me on television a couple of weeks before. And leading up to that television appearance, she was very enthusiastic. And there was a lot of phone calls, and letters, and contact. Then, after she saw me on television, that just stopped. And I think that, you know, she was majorly disappointed by reality. There was this fantasy and then there's reality. And I have to say, I was, too. When I first met her, she'd had an eating disorder in the past 12 months. She didn't look all that great. It was kind of strange when I met her because we'd organised where we were going to meet. And I was walking across the grass towards her, and she refused to turn around. Her adoptive brother was with her, and he'd seen me, and he indicated to her that I was coming across the grass. But she refused to turn around until I was almost right on top of her.

So I think by the time we actually got face-to-face [to] meet, she didn't want to meet. But she'd made this commitment she was going to meet and, so, she went through with it. But it was... the few times... I saw her a couple of times and they were, sort of, monosyllabic meetings.

Trauma for Life

Interviewer: Okay, I asked you this before, but how much of the emotional trauma that you still suffer is due to a fundamental heartbreak that you never got over?

Cameron: Okay, yeah. There's these two issues. I could say, "Okay, he's just pining because he lost the person he thinks was the love of his life." Or "there's this child." "There's this daughter," and that's the issue. The truth of the matter is this is not a death. Death's final. If my child, if my daughter, had died and if our relationship had disintegrated, you know, in some other way, then that's just as you say, "part of life." But death's final. Death's the cut off. Death brings that finality. But there's this part of me that's been amputated that's floating around out there in the world.

We are parents of missing children. No one would say to Lindy Chamberlain, "Oh, just pretend you never had an Azaria." No one would say to Tess Knight, "Oh, just pretend that Samantha never existed." We are the parents of missing children. And no one would ever dare say some of the things that get said to us, to parents like that. So, you know, I'm a parent of a missing child. I don't know where she is. I've had a reunion. I've seen her for five minutes in 32 years. I don't know where she is. I know she's living overseas somewhere. I don't even know exactly. I've pleaded with people to give me information. It's an amputation of a really important part of me. And yes, there's a memory of a love affair, and that's one thing. But there's an amputated part of me that is floating around in the world somewhere that I know nothing about – And I desperately want to know something about, because I had nothing to do with its removal. With her removal. It's like having a limb removed without your consent.

So, they're the issues. And they're the issues that get bigger and bigger and bigger, because there's more and more and more time that's been stolen from you. The issue for me is that, people say, "Oh, this happened 32 years ago. Get over it." You know? Well, my fathership over that girl wasn't just stolen from me 32 years ago. It was stolen from me yesterday. It'll be stolen from me tomorrow. It's this ongoing issue. And I have two other children and I know what it's like to be a father. And I know, you learn more about fatherhood and fathership and what actually was stolen from you. That's the issue. So, yeah, one thing's a memory, but, you know, the issue goes on because my fatherhood has been stolen today, tomorrow, and forever. It'll never be retained, it'll never be recovered. But at least there may be some time when I'll have a friendship with this person who's still living.

Not Allowed to Grieve

Cameron: So, for some reason, because someone else made these arrangements without my consent 32 years ago, I'm not allowed to miss my daughter. I'm not allowed to have a little grief. I'm not allowed to think about her every now and then. It's a double-standard.

We, as men, who've lost children to adoption, are only just now starting to get our voice. I don't know if I can say this to you, but I'll be surprised if this goes to air. And the reason I'll say that is because there have been other people who have tried to get these sorts of things to air, and they get stopped. Because no-one is listening. So if I go to the police, I feel very much that they're not going to take me seriously, for a start. And until there is some sort of social acknowledgement that there are illegalities. I have run this past lawyers, and they just freak out because they just go (and I haven't even had to get to the end of it) they've just gone, "Yeah. Yeah. Yeah. That clause means that. And that clause means that so, therefore, fathers should have been signing consents." And we've got 300,000 of these consents floating around Australia and not one of them that's got a father's signature on it. Now, okay, some of these men might have disappeared and couldn't be found. But the law states, you go find that guy and find out either what his attitude is, or you're supposed to get maintenance out of him (even for times before the child's born) and so on.

And until there's some awareness of this issue, that there are fathers out there that did try to stop these adoptions, and that there are legal arguments that are quite extremely compelling (and the other thing is that those legal arguments are never discussed when you talk to people involved in this issue). I mean, there's a whole Act they never talk about, because that's where all the grenades are...

Cameron Horn is an internationally-awarded writer with two master's degrees. He has a bronze medal and a "Best of Category" commendation from The New York Advertising Festival, is a six-time winner, and fourteen-time finalist, at The Australian Advertising Awards, as well as receiving numerous other university writing awards. He was a New South Wales Parliamentary Research Officer during the world's first Inquiry into Adoption in 1998. He subsequently authored *Rebecca's Law* (under the name Rohan McEnor), a novel based on evidence given to that Inquiry. In 2009, Cameron wrote one of the key research papers that forced the Australian Government to call a Senate Inquiry into Adoption. He is currently a writer for Southern Cross Austereo and lectures in Marketing and Advertising. Cameron is the father of a child removed for adoption.

---

[1] The interview was conducted in late 2012 by a reporter from The Australian Broadcasting Corporation. Allen Vance has reorganized and condensed this interview specifically for this anthology. The original interview transcripts can be found on the Origin's NSW website.

Our Stolen Son, Shane

THIS STORY NOT ONLY represents my own story, but can be representative of an estimated 150,000 mothers from Australia who lost their children to unlawful adoption from 1940-to-1998.

The photo of our son, Shane Stephan, was sent to me in May 1998, a fortnight after I found him. Thirty-one years had passed since the day he was stolen from me. Looking at this photo sent on the day before Mother's Day, it was hard for me to comprehend who the baby was, until I realized that this was my baby! There was an immediate trauma in realizing what was stolen from me a few short weeks from his theft and my release from prison. My first response was to go and hang myself from the awning attached to my home. In the photo, my baby was smiling into the face of a stranger. What more abuse could possibly be inflicted upon me?

My Story

On 16th February, 1967, just shy of my seventeenth birthday, I was taken from my bed, arrested, and imprisoned overnight at the South Brisbane Watchhouse. I appeared before the Children's Court the next day and was incarcerated at Holy Cross Wooloowin Brisbane for an indefinite period.

My crime? I was pregnant and was considered to be exposed to moral danger (even though I had a home of my own and the father of my child was prepared to marry me with our parents' consent).

Upon arrival at Holy Cross, I was locked up in the dormitory for four days without any contact with the other girls until bedtime. I hid under the blankets and pretended to be asleep when they came up. *I won't talk to them; this is all part of a dream.* I thought to myself that if I spoke to them, it would make what was happening to me real.

Four days later, I again appeared before the Children's Court (without counsel) and was then committed to Holy Cross indefinitely. Returned to Holy Cross, Sister Isobel, the head nun, handed me two straight white shifts and a pair of thongs that I was to wear and told me that, from now on, my name was to be "Leanne." I was told not to tell anybody my real name, nor was I to ask for theirs. After cutting my shoulder-length hair, I was taken down to the laundry where I was expected to work for the duration of my time in the home.

A week or so later, I was called into the office to sign papers to apply for my marriage. My fiancé had gone to Sydney to get our parents' permission to get married and, over the next few weeks, I lived in a state of hope, thinking every day that it was going to be the day that he would come and get me out.

Months later, hope and anticipation led to complete despair, followed by the realization that I was not going to be released. I can't explain exactly what happened but, at some point, something snapped inside my head and I went into a somewhat robotic state and *distanced* myself from what was happening around me. My brain was receiving *messages* that, if I was good and behaved myself, everything would be okay.

Although we were not verbally threatened by the nuns, there was always an underlying fear of being sent to a maximum security home, like Karalla. This deterred me from mixing with any of the state wards who were likely to cause trouble, the ones who were always sneaking around smoking, tattooing each other, fighting, and sexually abusing the younger, more vulnerable girls.

There were quite a number of break-outs whilst I was there, but they were always caught and brought back (or transferred to Karalla). The girls who had been to Karalla and sent back to Holy Cross told horrific tales of sleeping on the bare floors and food so rotten that it was inedible.

I constantly had thoughts of climbing over the three high fences and running away, but the thought of falling and hurting my baby scared me. One girl who tried broke her leg and was in plaster for months after.

For the next seven months, I did exactly what I was told. I cleaned, I worked five-days-a-week in the laundry, and I went to school. I wanted to show the nuns that I was a good girl and that I was going to make a good mother for my baby.

As my stomach got bigger and my pregnancy became more pronounced, I got more-and-more confused. Here I was at 17, locked up, and unmarried. Some mothers who resided in the home were about my age, if not younger. I became resentful and angry that they were allowed to come-and-go, rest when they were sick, and allowed to have visitors, and yet I was locked up because I was pregnant and unmarried.

The idea of discipline for the nuns was to inflict group punishment. If a number of girls were misbehaving, then everyone was punished. Visitations were cancelled and they would make us go to mass every day for weeks on end. The nuns seemed always to be hovering around us, their long black habits and white headdresses reminded me of circling vultures. They engaged in little conversation (unless to give orders), but were always praying, their long rosary beads constantly being fed through their fingers.

We became each others' jailers. If there was any misbehaviour, the small rewards we received from the nuns (like the 30 cent pocket money to buy sweets on Friday afternoon or a movie) were cancelled or revoked. A swimming pool in the rear of the home taunted us (only on special occasions were we allowed to swim in it to escape the hot Queensland weather).

Anyone who played up to the nuns or upset anyone was dealt with in the dormitory late at night. I was a model prisoner, older than all the other girls and pregnant, so I was left out.

Many nights were spent listening to the muffled sounds of the younger girls being sexually assaulted with hair brushes. I was too scared to speak out.

Any reference to sex was taboo, even the love scenes in the movies we watched were censored by a hand placed over the projector lens until it was over. I was put out of sight when the young boys from the local high school came to give dancing lessons to the girls on Saturday afternoons, making me feel dirty about my pregnant stomach (I was the only state ward in the institution with child).

Apart from working all day in the laundry, the days were made even longer by being woken up at five in the morning to go to mass. The long hours made me very tired and depressed. For eight months, I stood folding sheets, or dragging them tangled and wet out of the wire trolleys to bring them up to the rollers that pressed them flat. The only rest I got was when I was told to sit and fold pillow cases.

I was doing what I could to prepare myself for my baby. On the rare occasion that I got a visitor, I was given luxuries, like shampoo and talcum powder. These were saved for my baby in my locker on the back veranda. I had accumulated a little store of treasures and a work friend crocheted a little white matinee jacket and bonnet for the impending arrival. Every now and again I would look at them and imagine my little one wearing them.

It must have been a couple of weeks before I went in to labour when I discovered that my locker had been broken into and my treasured possessions were gone. I was devastated. Even though the other girls knew who had stolen my things, they would not tell me. The code of silence was never broken, not even by friends.

During the seven months of my incarceration, no one from the Children's Service Department (or the nuns) spoke to me about my baby. I was treated as if I wasn't even pregnant. In the last three months leading up to the birth, there were no visitors or letters. I felt as though the world had forgotten me. I learned later that my sister wasn't allowed to visit me for nearly four months before, or after, the birth of my child.

Months passed and the little person growing inside of me was my only connection to sanity. My baby was the only thing in that place that was real and, right up until I gave birth, I suffered severe heartburn and stomach upsets from the food. There was no medication given. Looking back, I see that the pain was a reminder that my baby and I were together.

At 6 A.M. on the first of September, 1967, I had a show in mass that morning. I was promptly packed off by ambulance to the hospital where I was admitted to the labour ward. After a number of hours without any contractions, a nurse came in and broke my water. I felt humiliated that my body was being invaded by metal objects. I was terrified that they were going to put something up inside of me to pull the baby out. It wasn't long after that the pains started.

I was in abject fear. No one came in to see what was happening to me as I watched the hands on the clock go 'round and around. I went into a state of sheer terror. The pains got stronger as I lay on the bed alone in the labour ward with not a word from a nurse or doctor to tell me what I was to go through.

Throughout the whole of my pregnancy, I was not given a piece of paper, booklet, or instruction about what might be involved. I was a terrified seventeen-year-old going through the traumatic sixteen-hour labour process with no idea of what was happening.

During delivery, I was treated like a piece of meat, never

spoken to (unless being given orders by the nurse) and I was tied to the side of the bed. My left leg tied up in a stirrup and my right leg pulled behind me until it felt as though my back was breaking whilst I was pinned down to the mattress. The sweet sickly smell of the gas and the rubber mask shoved on my face made me gag and reality drifted into a numbing unreality.

At 9:59 P.M., I gave birth to my son but, as I tried to turn over to see what was happening, the nurse again held me down until my baby was removed from the room. Struggling to see what was happening, I managed to catch a glimpse of a group of people leaving the room. *God! Were they watching me giving birth?* I felt as though I had been pack raped. When I asked what I had, I was later told that I had a son.

Due to the external and internal damage I had suffered during labour, I had to have stitches. The doctor who sewed me up joked about his herringbone stitch and compared his work to another doctor in the hospital. During this procedure not one word was said to me. It was as though I was a bag of garbage that wasn't worth acknowledging.

I hardly remember anything of the next seven days. All I can remember is the urgency to contact the father to let him know that I had had the baby. He came to the hospital to see me twice, but the whole thing is a blur. A flash comes of him, me, and his friend looking through the nursery window trying to work out which one of the babies was ours. Through strained eyes I was searching the rows of cribs. The father pointed to a black-haired child, "that must be him," we agreed. I was to find out later that my baby had blond hair.

My memories of the eight days spent in the hospital were mostly of hiding under the bed clothes. On the eighth day, a woman from the department came and threatened me with incarceration at Karalla House, telling me that my son would be put into foster care until I could prove that I could look after him. Immediately after signing the adoption papers, she asked me if I would like to see my baby (eight days after his birth!) and then gave me a card to hold up at the nursery window. I was shown a baby, but do not remember what he looked like. The sign over the cot read, "Baby McDonald, Not to be Shown."

When I have flashbacks, I just see myself standing at the window in a daze. I know now I was drugged and that was the reason for my dissociation.

After I had seen the baby, I was told to pack my things and was sent straight back to the home. It was as though I had never been away with not a mention of the baby. A nun ordered me to the laundry where I was to work until it was time for tea.

I spent the next six weeks in a dream-like trance. I had not had any visitors for almost four months, nor had I heard from my family. I felt as though I had been forgotten by the world and was going to be trapped forever.

Not long after my return to the home I was given a reward, of sorts. By not having a big stomach anymore, I was sent up to the convent to clean up after the nuns. Mother Liam commended me in front of the girls at morning prayers, saying that I cleaned the bathrooms better than anyone who had cleaned them before.

Six weeks after I gave birth to my son, I was told by a nun that I was being sent back to my mother in Sydney. I was angry. I had expected to be locked up until I turned eighteen, which would be in five months. Two days before my release, I was sitting on the veranda after work when Sister Isobel came along and ordered me to go to the laundry for the rest of the day.

I can remember telling her to "get lost" (my first act of defiance in nine months!) She started whipping my legs with a feather duster as I ran along the veranda and down into the laundry. I didn't care if they kept me locked up forever. There was nothing left for me in the outside world. I was released from the home six weeks after the loss of my son.

A few months later, whilst working in a lighting factory, a woman announced that she was leaving the next day as she was adopting a baby. I became upset. The birth and loss of my son came flooding back to me. I don't know why, but I went home and got the matinee jacket and bonnet a friend had crocheted for me and gave it to the woman at the factory. It was as though I was giving it to her for my own baby and the last physical connection with my baby was gone.

I spent the next thirty years living in a dream. Although I knew that I had had this experience, my memory of it was very hazy, like it had happened to someone else. I never spoke to anyone about it, nor did I tell my daughter about it (or the fact that she had a brother until she turned 19, some 23 years after the event).

When I finally found my son in 1997, I went through a period of happiness, depression, mood swings, and flashbacks.

I thought I might lose the plot entirely. I was in a state of utter turmoil and went to a psychologist who referred me to a psychiatrist. I had over 200 visits to the psychiatrist and came to the realization that, regardless of how much treatment, nothing could alter the damage caused by the theft of one's own child.

I am still in a state of trauma and anger 43 years later. I am still trying to come to terms with my imprisonment and the premeditated theft of my only son.

I initiated a case against the State of Queensland in 2004. My claim was dismissed by the Supreme Court, ruling that the matter happened too long ago to be tried now and that I had an unreliable memory due to the fact that I could not remember which day my son's father came to see me at the hospital. This contemptible judgment sent me into a suicidal state. *Why would a federal government allow any judiciary to cover up the crimes of its states against citizens of a commonwealth?*

They Stole My Future, They Stole Shane's Past

I have held my silence for many years since my reunion and, with the inspiration of other mothers who have shared their stories, I would now like to voice my thoughts on what I have lived though and observed during the past 13 years.

When I found my son in 1998, the full impact (and ongoing

effects) of his abduction were not evident to me until I started to know him. Ours is what most people would consider a "successful" reunion with regular contact, visits, and the exchange of gifts.

My son and his wife had two children when I first met him, a girl about ten and a boy about six. One would think that they were young enough for me to be introduced to them as their grandmother. This was not to be. I was asked by my son's wife not to tell the children about my relationship to them, regardless of how painful this was. I accepted her request and expected that, eventually, the children would know who I was.

A number of years passed and the reunion with my son, whilst accepting and respectful, still remained reasonably distanced. I understood that he had his own family and that I crashed into his life without warning, so it was up to me to give him the space to find where I fit into his circle of things and allow him to contact me when he had the time.

Going Back to the Beginning

The Freedom of Information Act went into effect 1990 and I waited with bated breath to apply for my son's information so that I could find my lost baby. I already had his details on a reunion register since his 18th birthday with the hope that, one day, he would come searching. How comforting to later find out that he never knew of my existence.

I found out that my son was told of his adoptive status at 6 A.M. on his way to work.

What a trauma to be told, "By the way, you are not our son. Sign a veto so that this woman won't find you because we don't know what sort of person she is." My son did what he was told (along with the other three children). Once again, their "secret" was safe and they could go back to playing happy families.

This, of course, was a fallacy, given that the whole street in which the children grew up knew they were all adopted but, yet, kept the secret from them (a reflection on a society that will collude on a grand scale to hide the truth).

So, Tim Anthony James, aged 23, ceased to be that morning. He was the son of a mysterious woman whom he had to fear, a woman who had abandoned him, a slut, a low life who gave birth to him only to abandon him to strangers. His then wife relayed to me later that, when he returned home that day, he looked ashen and like he was in a trance.

A magazine, called *That's Life*, printed the story of my search. This issue was seen by the adopters who revealed to my son (on the day I had found him) that they had seen the article 18 months prior and knew that I was the mother of the child they had adopted. They had read the story of how I was imprisoned and how he was taken and, yet, they spared not a thought for the poor desperate woman searching for her child. They could have saved me another 18 months of desperation.

When he told me this, I asked him, "Did they tell you I was searching for you?" His response was, "No."

So this was how the game was played. Not surprisingly, considering that he did not know of his adoption until he was 23, when the adopters confessed to the (now) four children that they were, in fact, the children of other mothers.

From what I gather, the adoptive family was shattered on these revelations and my son (the eldest), held the disenfranchised group together until the situation just reverted back into a state of denial.

The veto against me, pressured by the adopters, sent me into a tailspin, with a major breakdown and the eventual loss of my home, family, and friends. I walked out on my life in Sydney to live in Caboolture, Queensland, only a few kilometers from where my lost son lived. Imagine my despair in the knowledge that my granddaughter would be attending the school that I would have been working in and that my son drove past my house everyday on his way to work.

In the course of our conversations, he described Holy Cross Wooloowin brick-by-brick. *How did he know so much?* "The adoptive parents lived three doors down," he told me. "Did they know what went on in that place?" I asked him one day. "No, and they would have been too busy to think about it."

They lived so close to the hellhole that incarcerated me.

Imagine my horror (given they were Catholic!) and probably volunteered at the home and went to mass in the church we were forced to attend.

Our reunion progressed and, on fleeting visits to Queensland, I managed to see my grandchildren (whom, I assumed, still did not have any idea of who I was). From what I was told, they thought I was an "old friend from Sydney."

Years passed, but my relationship with them was (and *is*) lost. Adopters who were strangers to me were reveling in the joy of my grandchildren, whilst the children of my only child, Amanda, lost the only cousins, uncle, and aunt that they had.

It was only when my granddaughter felt that something was "not right" that she was told who I was (and, by then, she was old enough to leave home and start her own life). I believe that she eventually told her brother, but it was too late to recapture the lost years. I would never be able to take my rightful place as the mother of my own child, but I also lost my grandchildren to strangers. *How can this happen?* These strangers did not adopt my grandchildren or great-grandchildren!

I have been forced to sit in the audience of my son's life, watching a fictional story being played out in front of my eyes. The reality being that strangers are living my life as my child's mother and grandmother.

Over the past couple of years, I have been watching my grandchildren's lives develop via Facebook. My first great-grandchild was born two years ago and I watch his milestones from afar. I assume that I will also do this with my second great-grandchild. *Why is this?*

It is because these strangers, who have tacked my son on to their family tree, have also stolen my family name that cannot be passed on into the future through my son or any present, or future, grandsons.

My question is: Who the hell thought they had the right to displace my child and rob him of his identity? Why can a statutory authority falsify legal documents to reinforce the fraud committed by a breach of Common Law? My son has three birth certificates (only one of which is true).

My son, grandchildren, and great-grandchildren are not blank slates. They have a history of people who have struggled, fought, died, worked, and defended the freedom of others, and how dare anyone deprive them of the legacy of their ancestors?

I may have been silent for a long time, but I have seen too many of my dearest friends (mothers like me), depart this world with some of these words left unsaid:

For the theft of my only son — I am outraged.

For the knowledge that he lay untouched, unbonded in a hospital crib for 16 days before he was taken to be raised by strangers – I am outraged.

For the theft of my child's past, present, and future family history, identity, and destiny — I am outraged.

For the depersonalizing, brainwashing, and fraudulent life that was inflicted upon my son and his generation — I am outraged.

At the strangers laying claim to my past, present, and future — I am outraged.

When I hear my son call his adopters "mum" and "dad," I am diminished and belittled.

For each time that I've written my son's false name on a letter or card — I am disenfranchised.

For the times when I have flashbacks — I am traumatized.

For the knowledge that my son cost his adopters five dollars — I am incensed.

For the loss of my future—I am inconsolable.

And for the loss to my daughter, Amanda, and her six children who may never know their cousins, uncle, or auntie – I will continue to be outraged.

For the knowledge that those who took my son, and knowing that he would suffer serious problems of identity and abandonment – I will continue to seek acknowledgement of their negligence.

For those who entrusted my son to strangers and never bothered to follow up to see whether he was safe or well – I will continue to demand accountability.

For my son and his children's children – I will continue to seek truth.

In conclusion: To this day, my son's adopters have never uttered a word to me, nor I to them. Both of them believe that my story is not true and a landmark court case could not sway their conviction. From what I gather, they have not had any relationships with the other mothers of the children they adopted (other than a couple of fleeting meetings). His adoptive father died a few months ago and I could not offer any sincere sympathy to my son. I expect that my feelings will be the same if I outlive his adoptive mother.

It took the pain and suffering of four mothers to assemble this group of strangers and the result was far from ideal. *Was it worth it?* I am yet to be convinced.

Since 2003, **Lily Arthur** has been the New South Wales Coordinator of Origins Inc. For fifteen years, she has volunteered for the adoption community, focusing on people who have been forcibly removed or separated from their families, including those in the Aboriginal community. Since 1999, she has sat on the Stolen Generations Alliance as the NSW Non-indigenous Delegate. Lily is committed to fighting for justice for survivors of past policies and unlawful practices. Lily has also stood at two federal elections and at least ten State and Federal Parliamentary Inquiries. Closest to Lily's heart is bringing about an alliance of Australians Affected by Family Separation, including the Forgotten Australians, Stolen Generations, and Australians Separated by Forced Adoption. Lily's story is revealed in the documentary, *Gone to a Good Home*, while her defeat in a landmark court-case, Arthur vs. the State of QLD, did not divert her from campaigning for the rights of mothers and their lost children.

Bringing My Baby Home

At Home

I COULDN'T FUNCTION WHEN I got home from the hospital after giving birth to my second child, a son. I couldn't think, I couldn't do anything except feed my four-year-old daughter. I didn't eat regular meals for almost two weeks. I spoke to the adoption lawyer and asked, "Why was there never a legal contract made up for visitation rights?" Within a few days, I was sent a form. On the bottom of this form it stated that "this is not a legally binding contract." I started to panic. I felt betrayed. *Had I made the worst mistake in my life?* I suspected that I hadn't thought this through and that I might never see my son again. I sent an e-mail to the lawyer asking him to add my father so that he could have rights to contact and receive photos of my son. I was sent the same form reflecting my father's name this time. I started looking over all of my paperwork. I noticed the lies and deceit in some fine print: *An open adoption can be closed after my baby was legally adopted.* I decided to do some research and started looking online for support groups and made an appointment.

When Baby Was Born

On December 8, 2012, my son was born and my life changed and I thought I was ready to give (what some call) a "gift" to someone. I believed I couldn't mother two little ones and was ready to release my second baby to someone else. I had a bad experience in the hospital and was treated like white trash, but it was over and I was still alive. I believed (until my experience in the hospital), that I was saving my son and doing the right thing. Since then, I have changed my beliefs. When he was born, I had my doubts about his welfare. I didn't sign the 30-day waiver form and I was told my doubts were "just hormones." Twelve days later, I still felt the same way. I felt like a piece of me was missing. I couldn't go into stores or anywhere if there was a little boy present. Every day I woke up wondering what my day would be like if he was there. I wanted to go get him, but didn't because people seemed to be so concerned about the adoptive family. I didn't know what to do or who to talk to. Everyone who was involved in the legal aspects were on the side of the adoptive mother and the attorneys worked for the agencies. The attorneys say it's my hormones or post-partum depression that caused my depression, but it wasn't. I wanted my son home and I felt I would be making a horrible decision by relinquishing him for adoption.

After my baby was born, the adoptive mother communicated with me every day via e-mail, giving me updates and pictures. I, to this day, don't know what her true intentions were. (*Was she a concerned mother or just a great actress?*) She would tell me and the baby's father how my daughter and I were now a part of her family. I told her my concern about the threat of being kicked out of the house by my parents.

I Said, "No."

After two phone calls from a social worker, I told her, "I have changed my mind about releasing my baby for adoption." Once again, she tried to get me to believe adoption was best for everyone concerned, but she couldn't get me to change my mind. She was still trying to guilt-trip me, my so-called advocate, who proclaimed so hard that she was working for me was still pressuring me in the wrong direction. *It was unreal.* She was supposedly in my corner and would support what was best for me, but the adoptive mother had money and the social worker had to make a living. I told everyone I didn't want to give up my baby for adoption. I was pressured by the adoptive mother to go home and think it over. She even came into my room and asked me and I said, "No." A normal person would have walked out after that, but she stayed and told me that her heart would break if I didn't give her my baby. *All I wanted was my son.*

My Finances

I didn't care if I had to walk, I was going to get my son back. There was no way that this lady who lacked empathy, who lied about his name, and who acted like a monster in the hospital could be a better mother (richer maybe, but not better) than me. Finances can change. The baby and I were together for nine months. I wanted to be together in the future. I don't have much money. I have proven that I can be a good mother to my daughter. We'll get by. My mind was made up.

A Sense of Relief

After reaching out, I found a wonderful person who directed me to a woman who helped. She supported me and introduced me to people who could help me get my baby back. I was in contact with the social worker who had given me false information. I called Los Angeles County Social Services and was told that they were concerned. They asked me for the social worker's name and the names of everyone involved. They explained that this was not how things are done and that they were going to make some calls to those involved. I was told to watch what I said to the agency. I received a call from the social worker, who was in Nevada at the time, who appeared to be concerned for my safety. Everyone involved thought it was weird that I was going to pick my son up and told me to make sure that I had legal counsel close by.

The Journey Home

I was to pick up my son on Saturday, December 22, 2012 (fourteen days after he was born). Since my parents weren't living together anymore, my daughter went to stay with my dad and my wonderful mother took the journey to Northern California with me. I made arrangements for an additional witness to meet us up there so I wouldn't be by myself in the house, because mom had to stay with the car. When we got there, my stomach sank. I was welcomed in by a group of people who were all dressed alike. My son's adoptive mother was sitting on a couch holding him, not wearing any make up and looked unkempt and tired, as if she didn't realize how hard it was to raise a baby. I was focused on getting my son out of her arms because I had a sick feeling. The adoptive mother tried to tell me about his eye, and other things, but I knew I had to get out of there. I knew something was fishy and, if I hadn't had the additional witness, I think things would have been worse. They all stood on the porch and stared at us while we drove away, but I finally had my son back.

I learned something else from the trip: *My doubts about being the mother of two children was nothing compared to the reality of giving one of them away.* After seeing the adoptive mother, I have no doubt left that I am the better mother.

We drove for a few hours because I was scared. I thought the adoptive mother was up to something and wanted to get out of the county. His eye needed medicine, but she hadn't given me any. She did, however, give me diapers, but they were too small. He was on a formula used by the hospital that made him colicky. (I guess she didn't believe me when I told her how bad the formula had been for my daughter.) I had to take him to the hospital to make sure he was okay and to get his medication.

Home at Last

Now that my babies are together again, I will never let anyone pressure me into anything ever again. Now he will not grow up being neglected. Letting my son go (because I was not rich at the moment) was not in his best interest. My kids come first. I don't care what anyone thinks. Never make a choice that will negatively affect your child. There is help out there. You can get help. Now I have an army of supporters who are there for me and my kids. If it weren't for them and a few other people, my little baby son might still be missing, but because I wanted help and support, they helped without question.

I have since contacted the social worker who claimed to be my advocate. I asked her if she would send me my baby's medical records. Her response was, "I cannot assist you once you revoke the consent. You will need to call the hospital yourself. They have the birth records. My role, at this point, is over unless you decide to place again." I received a bill from the agency asking for over $19,000 in adoption-related expenses. A lawyer is still trying to get money from me. I received a bill from the adoptive mother claiming that I owed her a lot of money, as well.

It amazes me how a stranger can walk out of the hospital with a baby, but his real mom has to fight tooth-and-nail.

Reaching Out

I sent out over 200 e-mails and three responded. I wasn't expecting a response from anyone.

A wonderful lady who read one of my messages called right away and told me how she could help me, but all I could do was cry. I was scared because I had nothing for my son. These wonderful women told me that they would help with everything. I couldn't stop crying. All of these people who didn't know me suddenly wanted to help. She asked her contacts if they could donate baby items for my boy. The response was above-and-beyond what I could have expected. I had support from people I had never ever met. You name it, I got it. *Me!* I couldn't believe it. I have never met a group of such amazing women in my life. I now have incredible people helping me with lawyers and with obtaining medical supplies.

Kristina Laine was helped by a grassroots network of mothers of loss, adoptees, and even some temporary guardians who *get it* and are all focused on family preservation. Members have helped fifteen mothers over the last two and-a-half years to keep their families intact. They sponsored five families over the 2013 holiday with a "Sponsor a Saved Family" event, giving these mothers and fifteen children a Christmas to remember. When at all possible, **Lynn Johansenn** continues to build this network by providing some support for mothers and children who would not otherwise be able to find any real assistance from typical adoption "professionals." She invites others to contribute to her network, which can be found at "WsBirthmom" on Facebook.

PART 4: *Protected*

Stolen Lives

We were bought, yes, we were sold,
when we were but a few days old.
For what was called a "donation,"
a family got this new creation.

Oh weren't they great to take us on?
From fallen women we were gone,
Gone to have a better life,
free from trouble, free from strife.

Those who bore us would forget,
the child that they had barely met.
But life is seldom as it seems,
and ours are tainted by the dreams.
We dream about what might have been,
the kind of life we've never seen.
A woman that we can't quite see
and wondering, "Does she think of me?"

Who is my dad, who is my mum,
and if I found them would they run?
Or would it cause them too much shame,
the very mention of my name?
Nuns with their pockets, bursting at the seams,
and helpless mothers, desperate screams.
We were torn, from their arms,
inside the walls of baby farms.

You must pray, you must repent,
and here your time, it will be spent,
washing, scrubbing, ironing, too.
These are the jobs that you must do,
To try and wash away your sin,
and earn your freedom back again.
But our poor mums were never free,

not even an apology.

Now us, well we will always be,
the outcasts of society.
Under the carpet we were swept,
while our poor mothers wept and wept.
But on the horizon lies a new dawn,
and we shall all be reborn.

A bastard army ready to fight,
we are the beacon, we shine a light.
A light of hope to guide forever,
mother and child who should be together.

Colette Noonan

My Son to My Rescue!

"Keep on going, never stop growing." – Jenette Vance

I AM A KOREAN-BORN ADOPTEE and one of the Vance Twins. Thankfully, my sister and I were brought up together. Janine has been my greatest support, my stability, and the main reason I survived childhood. I have often thought that if I was forced to endure my adoption *without* her, I might have died (or even committed suicide). I believe many intercountry adoptees, also called "foreign adoptees," feel an immense sense of loneliness within their adoptive "forever families" (and even within the adoption community). Being adopted is a very isolating experience, yet we tend to hide this isolation. We are taught to appear "grateful," even if we are treated poorly. I seriously do not know how other Korean adoptees are able to survive the experience. I *do* know that with my sister, I am stronger. My twin has made me more resilient during our journey together.

I recently had a dream that we were in a haunted house and we got separated by a group of unfamiliar people. Their faces filled me with fear and I knew they were there to separate us. Somehow, I escaped without my sister. The separation scared me. My only goal was to find her and I wasn't willing to leave the property until I did. Standing at a distance from the house while surveying the grounds, I tried to think of my next move. Suddenly, I spotted her walking around the side of the house. Just seeing her made me feel normal and safe again. After I woke, I was surprised to feel so frightened and sick to my stomach at the thought of losing her.

I was seventeen when I became pregnant with my son, Dustin. My adoptive mother's immediate reaction was to advise me to give my son away for adoption (in order to make things right with her and the Lord). This coaxing started early in my pregnancy, but the thought of giving my son to a complete stranger sickened me to the core. Let me try to explain the depth of my love for my son. You know when the partner says that he, or she, loves you so much that he, or she, would even live under a bridge with you as long as you are *together*? That is the love I felt for my son, but a thousand times more powerful. I would live under a bridge with him as long as we could stay together. My adoptive mother thought I was a rebel, but I was acting naturally. *No way* would I give him to strangers so *others* could feel better about my pregnancy. I knew I would never be at peace with this decision, but she accused me of being stubborn and wrong. After she learned that I didn't even have plans to get married, she accused me of being sinful. Ultimately, she ended up "disowning" me from the family.

Once my son was born, a whole new world opened up to me. In fact, by keeping him, I was able to navigate away from social compliance and, instead, into a wonderful world of new discoveries with my own family and my newfound independence. I recognized myself in my children (I now have a son and a daughter). Sadly, I realized that if I ever walked past my own Korean mother (or other family members), I wouldn't recognize them. Instead of feeling like I had dementia, my life became much more memorable while watching my children.

Because I have them, I now feel rejuvenated, have more reasons to live, and am stronger and more confident about who I am as a person (despite my adoptive mother's early rejection). As my son grew up, my allegiance to her started to dissipate and now my loyalties have completely aligned with him (he is now twenty-three).

When he entered the world, I realized that, even though I was only eighteen-years-old at the time, that he was a valuable asset to me. Going to college, getting a good job right after graduation, and entering the medical field have allowed me to raise him independently. I believe mothers should never be led to believe that they are incapable of parenting based on who they are during their pregnancy. Life is always changing. Usually, things get better. If things get worse, we can ask for help. Raising a child involves risks and opportunities. Motherhood should never be stolen from a woman just because she is poor or she doesn't have a ring on her finger. This universal experience should not be taken away from any woman. And if she has already been negligent or abusive, then her children should *still* have the right to their extended family, to know their true identity, and their origins. Motherhood is a gift, one that becomes richer and more fulfilling every day. I've discovered that my children are the teachers and that we are learning about life *together*.

Because I will probably never know my own Korean mother, I wanted to hear from real mothers who have been separated from their children by adoption. This is part of the reason why I created a group with my sister called, "Adoption Truth and Transparency Worldwide Network." From the other mothers, I've learned about the propaganda techniques developed by adoption agencies in order convince the public that taking infants and children from their families is considered "in their best interest" and a form of "child protection." In my opinion, *the best interest of the child* means always being told the truth. Adoption agencies should *not* be given the legal jurisdiction to bury identifying information from anyone. The best way to avoid adoption trauma is to support the child's mother. If we do not acknowledge the cause, and just deal with the symptoms, nothing will change and we will continue to be faced with the life-long sentence of being separated.

The adoption industry has yet to invest in real families. Because of the astronomical revenues for their "services," adoption agencies have a financial incentive to break up families. Adoption is a man-made system, a business based on convincing vulnerable women that the "best" thing to do is to hand her child over to a stranger. Shaming inexperienced parents is the foundation of this business. Lowering young mother's self-worth and twisting the truth so severely that even the parents, and society as a whole, naively agree that separation is "in the best interest" for all involved (and deemed the most loving course of action) is both unethical and irresponsible.

The logical and least-expensive solution would be to encourage, empower, and educate mothers and young families. It might be a slow rate-of-return but, like planting seeds and nurturing them to grow, it will take time. Corporations want to make money now. Yet, a single mother armed with an education will be able to cut down on the number of adoptions, unemployment, dependency on tax-payers that come in the form of rising costs of social and mental health services, resulting in a more empowered society. Happy and healthy moms create happy and healthy families. Children will no longer be taken from the poor and offered to the rich. *My advice?* If you are a new mother, hold your babies tight with your head held high. Know that you are a strong capable woman. *You can do it!* I think separating a child from his, or her, parents is one of the worst crimes against humanity. It's a life sentence of pain and sorrow.

Since learning about unethical adoption practices, **Jenette Vance** co-created a social media group called "Adoption Truth and Transparency Worldwide Network," which has more than 6,000 members and continues to grow rapidly. She established "Against Child Trafficking USA," a 501(c)(3) educational organization that serves to inform the public about the unfamiliar side of intercountry adoption. Jenette's passion has always been to help individuals reach independence and attain their highest potential. She is a Reiki Master, clinical hypnotherapist, and has worked in the healthcare field since 1995. Jenette has three children, ages 25, 16, and almost two. Find her on Twitter @adoptiontraffic and online at *Adoptionland.org*.

Adoption:
In the Best Interest of Whom?

DISCUSSION ABOUT ADOPTION CAN be quite a complicated matter, especially if you, as an adoptee, highlight some of the flaws in the system. It is not unusual for adoptees to be labeled "angry" or "ungrateful" if they raise their voices in a manner which does not correspond with the notion that adoption is built upon charity. What often happens is that criticism is silenced either by outright dismissal or by claiming that it must stem either from a personal trauma or a wish for revenge against the adoptive parents. This dismissal, however, ignores some fundamental questions as to how and why adoption across borders occurs in the first place.

Social stigma and an uneven distribution of wealth are two of the primary reasons why a child is relinquished. Here it must be stressed that relinquishment does not necessarily mean a complete surrender of the child. It may simply mean handing over a child into the care of others in a time of distress, but with no intention of adoption (at least not in the way we understand adoption in the West). It is also worth taking into consideration that the majority of children who are relinquished do have, at least, one living parent. Therefore, it is necessary to ask if this is enough reason to take away a child from its mother and/or father with the intention of cutting off all ties forever?

It is time we start rethinking adoption, especially in the light of the recent documentary, *Mercy, Mercy*, which aired on Danish television in 2012. What is most remarkable about this narrative is that the agency in the film claims that it followed all legal procedures, yet it still chose to operate in a country (Ethiopia) which has not signed the Hague Convention. The practices of the adoption agency make it apparent that it is no longer about finding parents for orphans, but instead about finding children for clients. Additionally, what has not been brought up in this particular debate, is that the word "adoption" does not exist in any African language. Because of this, it can be very easy to manipulate parents into thinking they are working on the same page as the adoption agency even if they don't understand the meaning of the word at the core of the transaction.

Lies and deception are not new phenomena in adoption. For years, adoptees have been met with closed doors and secrecy if they wanted to find their parents. Those who do are usually assisted by an intermediary because agencies have no interest in bringing families back together. Once the adoption papers have been signed or, in many cases fabricated, the agencies move on to the next sale and the adoptee just becomes another statistic. One must also not forget that international adoption is extremely lucrative for the agencies who broker these deals.

In India, where I am from, international adoption began in the 1960s and peaked in the early 1980s. However, the death of a child in transit in 1982 made people start to question the practice of adoption abroad. It was also alleged that children were sold for $2,000 each in the US. Later, it was decided that at least half of children should be made available for in-country adoption. Here it gets a bit murky, though, because even when in-country adoptions were on the rise, there was still a vested interest in placing children abroad, despite the Guardian and Wards Act, which prohibits followers of non-Indian religions (such as Muslims, Christians, Jews, and Parsis) to legally adopt a child. Also, placement agencies receive large donations from foreign entities.

Many will probably claim that I romanticize an adoptee's home country without paying enough attention to all the social dilemmas that these countries are faced with. While I can admit that there are a great deal of challenges around the world, I have yet to see how international adoption has changed the social environment in any of those countries for the better. In India, for instance, it has done nothing to eradicate caste discrimination, to help unwed mothers, or to change the dowry system.

Casper Andersen was adopted at the age of three from the southern state of Tamil Nadu, India. He has a degree in Graphic and Technical Design and in Indian Studies. His engagement in adoption politics started in 2005. At that time, he also co-established a forum for Indian adoptees in Denmark. Today, it serves mostly as a tool for people from India to exchange personal stories and, sometimes, to meet with each other (whereas in the beginning it was much more political). Casper still occasionally operates as event planner for this group. His latest activity, however, has been joining a newly-established association in Denmark, called *Adoptions Polititisk Forum*. It was created as a protest movement by adult adoptees who all felt a more nuanced adoption debate was needed. Casper blogs at *Adopted from India*.

A Critique of Intercountry Adoption

Introduction

WHAT IS FUNDAMENTALLY WRONG with intercountry adoption is the imbalance in the power dynamic. White Westerners adopt children, while non-whites in non-Western countries relinquish and supply those children. Intercountry adoption is, in other words, a one-way traffic and not an equal exchange of children in need between countries. Since its inception just after World War II, when the supply of working-class children for domestic adoption started to run short, intercountry adoption has been the last resort for affluent infertile couples who feel a strong social pressure to fulfill the standard of the nuclear family. Intercountry adoption is widely perceived as a progressive and anti-racist act of rescuing a non-white child from the miseries of the Third World, something which legitimizes the practice in the first place. This bizarre situation is loaded with demands of loyalty, guilt, and gratefulness as the wealthiest of the rich in the receiving countries adopt the most shunned and unwanted in the Third World.

Historical Prerequisites

Before World War II, no Westerner thought about adopting a non-white child. Racism was the order of the day in the colonial world order at a time when the West ruled the world. Before the war, different humanitarian organizations actually tried to place Jewish refugee children from Central Europe, via *Kindertransport*, into Swedish homes. Today, we can read about the difficulties in placing those children in letters preserved at the National Archive of Sweden: "We don't want Jewish children. Aren't there any Aryan children? "

How could Westerners be prepared to adopt "non-Aryan" children from Korea then at the beginning of the 1950s? The answers lie in the Holocaust and in decolonization. The scope of the Holocaust created such a shock that the West was forced to change its worldview. The West realized that the Holocaust couldn't just be a German issue and, instead, that all Western countries were "guilty" after 2,000 years of anti-Semitism. The West went abruptly from overt racism to the idea of equality for all races (at least theoretically). This idea destroyed the world order that dominated the last 500 years: Namely, that the West had the right to conquer, exterminate, and rule over non-white people. Decolonization was followed by violent conflicts and then the first intercountry adoptees started to arrive.

The Korean and Swedish Cases

The Korean War was not just a Korean war. It was a cynical and dirty war between the super powers that happened to take place on the Korean peninsula as the two Korean states were used as pawns in a game played by two Western powers. Representing over 10 percent of the combined population, 3.5 million Koreans were killed on both sides. The Korean War is considered one of the bloodiest in history (considering the limitation in time and in geography) with losses corresponding to one-fifth of the total global war casualties since World War II.

During the war years, soldiers from the UN-army started to adopt children. The UN-army contained representative members from most of the countries which would adopt the majority of the Korean children sent overseas: Australia, Canada, Luxemburg, the United States, Belgium, the Netherlands, France, Sweden, Norway, and Denmark. Witnesses describe the Korean War as something close to genocide. The UN-soldiers killed tens of thousands of Koreans indiscriminately on both sides and it is important to bear in mind that almost all of the first Korean adoptees were products of unequal relations between UN-soldiers and Korean women.

This same pattern followed in other countries. Decolonized countries, like India and Ethiopia became supplying countries as a consequence of international aid efforts (especially in East Asia). The Korean situation became the standard. Wars and catastrophes in countries like Vietnam and Thailand resulted in intercountry adoption from those countries. Worth noting is that many leading supplier countries in the field of intercountry adoption fall under America's sphere of military influence or have been subjected to American warfare: Korea, Vietnam, Thailand, and the Philippines in Asia, and Colombia, Chile, and Guatemala in South America.

Sweden played an important role all over the world, the result being that Sweden has brought in the largest number of adoptees among all Western countries (relative to the native population) with almost 45,000 from 130 different countries. After a pro-Nazi war history and a long tradition of racial thinking, self-righteous Sweden wanted to be a paradise for human rights, democracy, and anti-racism after 1945. Another less-idealistic motive worth mentioning was the sudden disappearance of adoptable Swedish children from the marketplace during the decade following the war as a result of rapid economic growth and an increased participation of women in the labor force, coupled with the development of an advanced social welfare system. Most important is Sweden's self image as the world's most democratic country, a self-image recently challenged by the sudden appearance of a vigorous National Socialist movement and racism towards non-Western immigrants (including adoptees). Intercountry adoption in Sweden is nothing less than a national project to uphold this self-image.

For countries like Korea, the nearly insatiable demand for children has created huge social problems. Intercountry adoption has destroyed all attempts to develop an internal social welfare system, and the position of the Korean woman has remained unchanged. The Swedes have been forced to accept unwed mothers for a long time, but the children born out-of-wedlock in Korea, instead, disappear abroad. In the 1970s, during the golden age of Korean adoption when Korean children (like pets and mascots) became status symbols among progressive whites, the pressure was enormous in Korea to find adoptable children. Temporarily-relinquished children in institutions, and those who simply got lost from their parents on the streets, disappeared forever from the country. Intercountry adoption was also linked to the amount of money Western organizations gave to the institutions. The more children that were exported, the more money they received.

The consequences of intercountry adoption for supplying countries, in terms of a national trauma for the biological parents left behind, are today obvious in a country like Korea, the country that has sent away the largest number of children (more than 150,000 to 15 Western countries). Interestingly, Swedish documentaries on intercountry adoption always focus on the positive side, while the corresponding Korean documentaries always focus on the negative aspects.

"The Best Interest of the Child"

The expression "in the best interest of the child" is used as a mantra by proponents of international adoption. It is a fact that intercountry adoption has always worked in the interests of adoptive parents and receiving countries and never for the interests of adopted children (or their supplying countries). If everything were truly "in the best interest of the child," then siblings would never have been separated, and every adoptive parent should have been forced to travel to the supplying country to pick up the child and, at least, attempt to learn something of that child's actual language and culture.

In 1969, during a visit to Sweden, Mr. Talk, the director of Social Welfare Society (SWS), a former adoption agency, said the following regarding "the best interest of the child": "We have to realize that Korea is not forced to give away children for adoption. We have to think about the children in the first place, not the parents. It would be better to find individual homes in Korea for these children." The last method is apparently considered to be "in the best interest of the child" for white children in the West, however, Swedish foster children are not adoptable at all. Swedish children and Korean children are simply not treated as equals on the world stage.

Adoptive parents have the right to choose between age, country, race, handicap, et cetera. The fact that some countries have been favorites for adoptive parents says a lot about how much racial thinking still continues to live on just below the anti-racist surface. Korean, Ethiopian, and Colombian children can more easily pass as whites (relative to other countries in the same regions). Furthermore, adoptive parents in Sweden seem to have a clear preference for girls and "racially pure" children. (Non-white girls are probably less threatening, especially for infertile men.)

Paternalistic and neo-colonial thinking considers adoptees to be eternal children. We are forced into the role of adopted children throughout our entire lives. First and foremost, we are Swedes (as we are not allowed to explore our actual ethnic origins). In spite of this total lack of respect towards the adopted child, the adoptive family continues to act the prescribed "mother, father, and child" roles even if this social anomaly can never develop into a biological relationship. *Is it a right to take other peoples' children?* Only an upper middle-class citizen can answer this question in the affirmative.

Parallels to Slavery

The West has a long tradition of uprooting non-whites and transporting them, involuntarily, to their own countries and for their own purposes. Hundreds-of-thousands of non-whites, especially Africans, were transported to the Americas to satisfy the need for labor. Nowadays, thousands-upon-thousands of non-whites, especially East Asians, are transported to the West to satisfy the needs of infertile white middle-class couples. The message of intercountry adoption is clearly that life in the West is the best, and that the West has the right to adopt children from non-Western countries in the name of paternalistic humanism and materialistic superiority, reminiscent of the pro-slavery arguments from the 19th century: By leaving war-stricken and impoverished West Africa, the slaves were given a better life in the New World.

Contemporary intercountry adoption has flown in close to half-a-million Third-World children to the West during a period of fifty years has many parallels to the Atlantic slave trade which, between 1440 and 1870, shipped 11 million Africans to America. Similarly, 12 million Indians and Chinese were dispatched to the European empires between 1834 and 1922. However, a crucial difference is, of course, that the slave trade and indentured servitude are today almost universally condemned, while intercountry adoption is still in operation, perfectly accepted by Western societies and legalized through various international conventions.

There are indeed numerous striking similarities between the slave trade and intercountry adoption. Both practices are demand driven, utilizing a highly-advanced system of pricing and commodification of human beings, as well as being dependent on the existence of intermediaries (in the form of slave hunters and adoption agencies) and a reliable system of transportation. Both the African slaves and the Third World children are stripped of their identities as they are separated from their parents and siblings, Christianized through baptism, stripped of their language and culture and, in the end, branded or given a case number.

The so-called "House Negroes" in America must be the closest parallel to intercountry adoptees as both are forced to live with their masters, treated like their children, and legally part of the household. And, last-but-not-least, both groups are brought over only to please and to satisfy the needs and the desires of their well-to-do buyers (slave owners and adoptive parents, respectively).

Cultural Genocide and Racism

We had to give up our Korean identity when we arrived in Sweden, and it doesn't matter whether we were five-weeks, or seven-years, old. We were emptied of our Koreanness and filled up with their Swedishness. One effect of this is that few adoptees remember their childhoods in their home countries. Everything un-Swedish is considered "forbidden." We arrived in Sweden on Swedish conditions. Everything linked to Korea is taboo or slandered and Korea, itself, is contemptuously considered to be a "bad" and "poor." Many adoptive parents have strange fantasies about Korea that often have strong sexual undertones: "your mother was a prostitute," "you are a child of incest," and "if you were in Korea today, you would either be dead or a prostitute."

The adoptive parents want the adopted children to feel "chosen," but, in reality, adoption is nothing but a grim lottery. On top of all of this is the expectation from the adoptive parents that we feel eternally grateful, loyal, satisfied, and happy. The truth is that we would never have been here in the West without 500 years of colonial history or without the dominant ideal of the middle-class nuclear family.

When the adoptee leaves the adoptive family to become an adult, the immigrant identity is imposed. From a privileged adopted child with adoptive parents who fight to make their adopted children believe that they are "special" (i.e., not immigrants), the adult adoptee becomes just another non-white immigrant. That is the African-Americans' strongest opinion against interracial adoption: white parents can never teach their non-white children survival strategies for living in a racist society. A similar argument was heard from some African countries refusing to participate in intercountry adoption in the 1970s: "You don't treat our children with respect and dignity."

However, these arguments have rarely reached global policy makers. Instead, it is assumed that there are no special emotional or psychological problems or costs of being a non-white adoptee in a white adoptive family living in a predominantly-white society. Consequently, assimilation becomes the ideal as the adoptee is stripped of his or her name, language, religion, and culture as the bonds to his or her own family and country of origin are systematically cut off. Adoptees who consciously dissociate themselves from their country of origin and see themselves as whites are seen as examples of successful adjustments, while any expressed interest in cultural heritage or biological roots is seen as an indication of poor mental health. Recently, proponents of intercountry adoption have also started to attack the "politically correct" ban on interracial adoption.

The structural racism against non-whites, of course, also affects adoptees. It is important to remember that tens-of-millions of white Europeans today often vote for openly racist candidates with strong National Socialist leanings. I feel that we are "stranded" here in the West in an aggressive and arrogant culture that treats us like animals.

To feel subordinate is not only the adoptee's experience. There are some parallels to second-generation immigrants and to people of mixed blood. Members of these groups, however, can find strength in cultural identities that we are completely denied by way of adoption. The question is not: "Am I a Swede or am I a Korean?" The question is rather: "How can I survive as a marginalized East Asian in Sweden?" To be a Korean adoptee is to live outside of both cultures. We will never be considered Swedes and we cannot return to Korea due to legal, linguistic, and cultural barriers.

Orientalist Imagery

Racism against East Asians is still an acceptable racism so much that it doesn't even count as racism. Racism against East Asians is ridicularization and collectivization. We are ugly, fussing, and something to laugh about. We are outsiders, Martians, numerous, tiresome, subservient, idle, and impossible to tell apart. Our unique situation as both adoptees and as non-whites (who have grown up with whites) make us especially sensitive to racism. We have lived, slept, and eaten with the "enemy."

The stereotyped sex roles are disastrous for East Asians. The feminization and infantilization hit both sexes and have direct consequences on our daily lives. East Asian men are desexualized and are attractive only for some homosexual men or pedophiles. East Asian women are, on the other hand, hyper-sexualized in a way that has little to do with actual sexuality. It is rather a question of power and violence with strains of pedophilia.

This pattern is the norm in the United States. Ever since arriving in the 19th century, Asian-Americans have had strong difficulties building their own stable communities. Asian-Americans have the highest ratio of interracial relations, a fact that concerns Asian women, particularly. In some generations and ethnic groups, as many as 80 percent of the Asian-American women have left their own community for white men.

Every year, tens-of-thousands of white men (many of whom are academics in Asian Studies) travel to East Asia to find wives and they make no differentiation between countries like Korea or Thailand. East Asia is, for many white men, just one enormous sexual fantasy. These white men are tramping in the same footsteps as their heroes, the American soldiers who raped East Asian women and killed Asian men in countries like Korea, Laos, Vietnam, Cambodia, Thailand, Taiwan, the Philippines, and Japan. These sexual fantasies have their own pornographic genre, called "Asian girls," a category showing strong pedophilic influences.

White views about East Asians have been taken for granted, especially among adoptees. The men feel ugly, while the women feel "special" and interpret the totally unselective attention from white men as complimentary. The men remain bachelors while the women marry white men (which might have something to do with basic survival instincts: being married to a white man is, honestly speaking, a one-way ticket into the white society).

Outcomes of Intercountry Adoption

Studies on adoptees have been conducted ever since the first children started arriving in their host countries in the 1950s, and the majority have been qualitative works based on small groups of children or adolescents with adoptive parents as informants that focused on issues of attachment, adjustment, and self-esteem. In North America, Scandinavia, and Western Europe, the field is heavily dominated by researchers who are either adoptive parents themselves or affiliated with adoption agencies. Because of these obvious limitations, the outcomes of studies are, almost without exception, interpreted as positive. Any problems that have been identified are attributed to a combination of pre-adoption and genetic factors as it is understood that there couldn't possibly be any difficulties at all with being a racial minority. Unsurprisingly, there are few studies on adult adoptees and few quantitative population studies, while the politically sensitive issues of race and ethnicity are mostly dealt with in a superficial way.

However, new research has come to light, based on responses from thousands of adult intercountry adoptees in Sweden from quantitative register studies that show a less-positive picture of intercountry adoption. Antecedents to the Swedish studies were conducted in the Netherlands in the 1990s showing high frequencies of behavior and emotional problems among adolescent intercountry adoptees compared to their non-adopted control groups. The new Swedish studies, by far the most extensive ever conducted on intercountry adoptees in any Western country to date, clearly indicate that intercountry adoption is not as unproblematic and idyllic as it generally perceived.

The adult intercountry adoptees were selected from population registers and compared to equivalent control groups among ethnic Swedes. The results show that the group has had substantial problems in establishing themselves socio-economically (in terms of level of education, labor market achievement, and family creation) in spite of having been adopted, predominantly, by couples belonging to the Swedish elite. It is estimated that 90 percent of adoptive parents belong to the upper and middle classes. In spite of this, 6.6 percent of the intercountry adoptees had a post-secondary education of three years or more compared to 20 percent among the biological children of the adoptive parents with whom they grew up. 60.2 percent of the intercountry adoptees were employed compared to 77.1 percent of ethnic Swedes (with half of the former group belonging to the lowest income category compared 28.6 percent for the latter). 29.2 percent of the intercountry adoptees were either married or co-habitatating compared to 56.2 percent of the larger population. Intercountry adoptees often have less children. Those who are parents are more likely to live without their children if they are men or are living as single parents if they are women (thus, sadly, mimicking their biological parents' behaviors). Men are more likely than women to have indicators of social maladjustment.

Moreover, epidemiological studies show high levels of psychiatric illness, addiction, criminality, and suicide compared to the control groups. The probability of psychiatric hospital care was found to be 3.2, for treatment for alcohol abuse 2.6, and for drug abuse, 5.2. The probability of severe criminality leading to imprisonment stood at 2.6 and, for suicide attempt, at 3.6. Women have higher rates of negative mental-health indicators than men. The most shocking finding is a record high probability of 5.0 for suicide compared to ethnic Swedes, in an international perspective comparable only to the staggering suicide rates registered among indigenous people in North America and Oceania, which makes parallels to cultural genocide ghastly topical.

In this perspective, it becomes more evident than ever that intercountry adoption was nothing other than an irresponsible social experiment of gigantic measures from the very beginning.

Tobias Hübinette is a reader in intercultural studies at Södertörn University and a researcher in critical race and whiteness studies at The Multicultural Centre. Publications include: *Comforting an orphaned nation* (2006), *Adoption med förhinder* [*Adoption with obstacles*], co-authored with Carina Tigervall, in 2008, and "*Om ras och vithet i det samtida Sverige*" ["On race and whiteness in contemporary Sweden"] (2012). Tobias is a researcher, teacher, and political activist working for social justice and reconciliation for all parties who are involved with international adoption from Korea, including the adoptees, their parents, their spouses, and their families. In 2007, he was instrumental in founding "Truth and Reconciliation for the Adoption Community of Korea." In order to accomplish the goals of this organization, and those of his academic interventionism, he has focused on producing and disseminating knowledge that serves the social-justice movement comprised of adoptees and their allies.

Ireland's Banished Mothers

Background

WHEN THE IRISH FREE STATE was founded after the War of Independence and a brief civil war in 1922, the Catholic Church already owned and ran a network of institutions to deal with all aspects of social life in Ireland. Industrial schools, public primary and secondary schools, hospitals, Magdalene Laundries, and mental hospitals all fell under the Catholic Church's control as they finally won the sectarian war for converts and souls which had been raging with the Protestant Churches since about 1800. The "problem" of single, unmarried mothers was dealt with by a network of church-run institutions which existed across the country. By far, the largest was Saint Patrick's Mother and Baby Home on the Navan Road on the outskirts of Dublin. Over the years, homes of various sizes (from large converted Manor Houses down to privately-owned nursing homes in mid-sized terraced houses) existed as need dictated across the country. Sinners would be hidden behind high walls. People with special needs, orphans, even high-spirited teenagers, and minority groups, became *de facto* prisoners of a deeply judgmental, self-righteous, and arrogant church obsessed with sex (and its regulation).

The Sisters of the Sacred Hearts of Jesus and Mary arrived in Ireland in 1922 within months of the end of the civil war. The Order claims it was invited across from its headquarters in England by the newly-formed Irish Government to deal with unwed mothers. The nuns bought a 210-acre farm in Bessborough, County Cork, and began operating a Mother and Baby Home. The Order expanded in 1930 when they bought Conville House and grounds in Roscrea, County Tipperary, which they renamed "Sean Ross Abbey." In 1935, they bought the third (and last) of their homes; the old Manor House in Castlepollard, County Westmeath, with over one-hundred acres of land.

In that same year, Eamon de Valera had been serving as Taoiseach (Prime Minister) for three years. De Valera was a deeply conservative and devout Catholic who had seriously considered joining the priesthood during his late teens and early twenties. He firmly believed in absolute obedience to the will of The Church. When the Sacred Heart Sisters applied for a large grant from the Irish Hospital Sweepstakes, it was issued without question. The nuns used it to build Saint Peter's, a three-story, 120-bed maternity hospital. The Order also converted The Manor House into a convent with living quarters and offices and added a small chapel (Saint Joseph's) between The Manor House and hospital which was attached by a corridor to the side of their convent. De Valera's government also gave the sisters a "conversion grant" of £65,000 (a huge sum of money at the time). It is not known what The Sisters of the Sacred Heart did with this money as Saint Peter's was custom-built as a maternity hospital (despite the fact that they never bought any medical equipment or drugs of any description). Cheap cots, beds, tables, and chairs were the only furniture and the austere ornamentation consisted of religious statues.

De Valera let it be known to The Church hierarchy in 1940 that he would be pleased to see his friend and colleague from Blackrock College, Holy Ghost Priest John Charles McQuaid from Cootehill in County Cavan, promoted to the position of Archbishop of Dublin and Primate of All Ireland. McQuaid held the post from 1940 to 1972. Under his rule, The Church's worst qualities of that era grew steadily and it became deeply authoritarian, arrogant, sectarian, and misogynistic. McQuaid and de Valera formed a mutual partnership with the intention of turning Ireland into a conservative Catholic country which would shine forth as a beacon to the rest of a world falling into Godlessness and Communism. In the manner of a Faustian pact, de Valera used the church to build his political power base while McQuaid underwrote or approved acts of repressive social legislation, such as the Dance Halls Act, the Registration of Nursing Homes Act, and the Criminal Justice (amendment) Act (which banned contraceptives). De Valera personally owned and controlled the largest newspaper group of the time, The Irish Press, Plc, while his government ran the only Irish radio station. Censorship was strict and pervasive. They divided the country up into their respective spheres of influence. The Catholic Church ran the social lives of the people while the government ran the secular state dealing with issues like external relations and transport. The two men were also responsible for the ethos of the staunchly Catholic-leaning Irish Constitution (passed in 1937) and its anti-women's rights articles. In 1944, McQuaid had sanitary tampons banned for fear that "young women's passions might be aroused by the use of these new devices." These two deeply conservative Catholics, during separate and overlapping reigns, ruled for nearly forty years and, essentially, turned Ireland into an authoritarian theocracy. From 1932 until well into the late 1960s (when their power waned in the face of social liberalism), Ireland saw its critics' predictions become reality as Home Rule became Rome rule. For a considerable portion of their reign, approximately one percent of the Irish population was effectively imprisoned in various types of institutions, ranging from orphanages and industrial schools to Magdalene Laundries and mental hospitals; more than any other country in the world (holy Catholic Ireland pushed Stalinist Russia into second place). Before this era, James Joyce had referred to Ireland and its relationship with The Catholic Church as "Christ and Caesar hand in glove." McQuaid and de Valera brought this closeness to an unprecedented level, each running their own little state-within-a-state. In the early 1960s, McQuaid commissioned an American Jesuit, Father Biever, to carry out a survey of public opinion. He reported back to McQuaid that Ireland was "virtually a theocracy in which all significant legislation was vetted in advance by the clergy." (Coogan, p. 734) The government paid The Church generously for its services while the population was reduced to hunger, poverty, and mass emigration. During the 1950s, roughly 40,000 people left every year.

Saint Peter's served as a Mother and Baby Home (a maternity hospital for single mothers) for thirty-five years. Expectant mothers nearly always arrived at Castlepollard accompanied by their mothers and carrying a letter of reference from their local parish priest. Girls were stripped of their names and clothes as soon as their mothers left, their hair was clipped short, they were given rough uniforms and heavy wooden shoes/clogs, and assigned a "house name." They were ordered not to talk to one other.

The Sisters arrived to wake the girls before dawn every day and they would begin the daily routine of prayers and rosaries which carried on almost all day until bedtime. A quick wash in cold water preceded fire-and-brimstone sermons during daily mass. Pride and vanity were the enemy. Temptation, lust, sins of the flesh, mortal sin, and the seven deadly sins were the topics of endless lectures from the clergy. Many of the inmates, however, were victims of rape or incest. Some were housekeepers who were incarcerated because of a priest's behavior toward them. Pregnant girls often fainted during mass and were punished for their "insolence" and "disrespect."

Denied even the comfort of each other's friendship and companionship during the day, the girls worked in silence or to the sound of prayers being endlessly repeated by The Sisters. The young women were consistently underfed and almost universally refused even the most basic levels of healthcare and medical attention. They were not allowed to wear bras that would protect their sensitive nipples. Their pubic hair was shaved once a week by the mid-wife.

The Mother and Baby Home at Castlepollard never employed a doctor or nurse, as far as is known, but rather just one mid-wife at time. The qualifications and experience of these mid-wives are disputed, with considerable anecdotal evidence that they were unqualified or semi-qualified mothers who had given birth at Saint Peter's and just stayed on. At least one of them, Nurse Smith, had a dreadful reputation. All births were strictly natural. No painkilling drugs, gas, or air was ever used or allowed. No screaming or shouting was allowed. Sisters would regularly turn up during the delivery asking questions such as, "Was it worth the five minutes pleasure?" and generally mocking and verbally abusing the women and girls during their respective labours. Antibiotics were never used. Stitching a girl who was torn after a difficult birth was not allowed.

Another practice of The Sacred Heart Sisters in Castlepollard was to bully mothers into force feeding their babies solid food after only six weeks. At Sean Ross Abbey, nuns were forcing mothers to breast feed their babies for a full year to save money on baby food. Conditions varied according to the whims of the Reverent Mother in charge.

Some of the women were offered "posts" at the hospital as children's nurses and told they would be properly trained as pediatric nurses in the future. None ever received any formal training during, or after, their stay. Some of the girls washed, cleaned, dusted, and waxed the buildings. Most worked on the farm or in the commercial laundry attached to the back of the hospital. The girls were expected to stay for about two years to repay the cost of their "room and board," although many stayed with their children for up to four and, in some cases, even five years. Forcing vulnerable girls to pay off fictional debts is the same tactic employed today by human traffickers who enslave innocent girls as sex slaves.

The Sacred Heart Sisters, as with all other Catholic institutions, made vast profits as they operated with unpaid labour. The entire Church and all of its institutions were completely tax-exempt. Saint Peter's laundry was done by hand, but when The Sisters could find local contracts, they took in the washing at full commercial rates. Alongside the Magdalene Laundries, Castlepollard and Sean Ross, almost certainly, had local government contracts (although no definitive proof of this has as yet emerged). The girls worked the farmlands of over 300 acres in Bessborough and Castlepollard. The produce was sold on at full-market value while hungry, pregnant girls saw none of the (literal) fruits of their own labours. At one time, the local authorities paid The Sisters sixteen shillings per mother, per week, and two shillings and-six-pence per baby, for their care. The Sacred Heart Sisters, as well as most of The Catholic Church, pleaded poverty and lobbied the government for more money. They always had advanced warnings of inspections and gave the homes a makeover before any officials arrived onsite. However, on the rare occasions when a government inspector would actually confront the religious orders about conditions in any of their institutions, they used government "under funding" as a ready-made excuse. The government subsidy was used to buy the cheapest margarine to be had that was then spread on bread and handed to the girls as one (or two) of their daily three meals. Bessborough had its own Farm Shop to sell its produce at full-market value. The girls were allowed two eggs per week. The Sisters also solicited and received, generous "donations" from natural and adoptive families, usually amounting to multiples of weekly earnings. Well-off families who could afford to pay, "donated" £100 for private care and a speedy exit (they were often in-and-out in as little as six weeks). The Church, like the entire country itself, was deeply class ridden at the time.

Saint Peter's Hospital in Castlepollard is a grey, dull building designed by T.J. Cullen (1879–1947). It was built back-to-front. As you come up the driveway to The Manor House, the back of the hospital appears on your left and is covered with pipes. The laundry extension sticks out. On the opposite side, the facade is plain, but respectable. It was built this way to further emphasize the girls' collective shame. Babies were kept in wards on the ground floor while mothers stayed on the second floor in dormitories. The third floor had two large, bare rooms at the back where all the births took place with mums and newborns remaining on the third floor for two-to-six weeks after birth. The girls from well-off families also stayed in their rooms on the third floor, but were excused from work. People who adopted children often spoke of their underdevelopment when they collected them. The children were noticeably months behind the norm in speech and walking skills due to lack of attention. This was common with all children adopted from Catholic Mother and Baby Homes. The Order of the Sacred Heart Sisters referred to the babies as "bastards" and "illegitimate," but their particular favourite was "the spawn of Satan." The co-founders of Adoptee Rights Now were born in Castlepollard and Sean Ross Abbey.

Numerous records show the nuns in both Mother and Baby Homes and Magdalene Laundries phoned Gardai to recapture runaways and the *Gardai* dragged them back to their prisons. The local station in Castlepollard is directly across the road from the main entrance to Saint Peter's. After being returned to the home, they were locked into a room on the ground floor as punishment and often beaten. Their hair was clipped to almost nothing, or sometimes, roughly shaved. The Sacred Heart Sisters remain steadfast at the time of writing (2013) that girls voluntarily entered, and remained in all three of their Mother and Baby Homes. (In fact, all of the orders of nuns involved in adoption remain adamant that the inmates in their institutions entered and remained there voluntarily.) But even if this fantasy were true, how can the issue of whether the inmates were prisoners or not possibly negate the nuns' and the Church's duty-of-care towards vulnerable pregnant girls and their babies? There is no excuse for starving pregnant women and denying them medical treatment and equipment or neglecting their babies to death.

The little chapel in Castlepollard, Saint Joseph's, saw at least fifteen marriages over the years. If a boyfriend of one of the girls showed up, the Reverent Mother would simply say, "Right! No time like the present," send for the priest, and have the couple married on the spot. After a cup of tea and a slice of cake the happy couple was shown the door.

Ireland's Banished Babies

Two hundred and seventy-eight babies from Castlepollard, born between 1948 and 1973, were sent to America, or about one-in-four. They are known as the "Banished Babies." This practice began when American airmen, stationed in England after World War II, discovered how easy it was to adopt babies in Ireland, compared with the far stricter American system (which also had a very limited number of babies available for adoption). The Castlepollard Banished are among a total of, at least, 2,132 babies and young children who were effectively sold to rich American Catholics by The Sisters with the assistance of the Minister for External (Foreign) Affairs Eamon de Valera. De Valera illegally issued passports to the exports on the orders of Archbishop McQuaid and the nuns. This was child trafficking on an industrial scale. Some fifty babies of this total were sent to countries such as England, Germany, Libya, Egypt, the Philippines, India, Australia, South Africa, and Venezuela. The furor caused among senior civil servants at De Valera's issuance of passports at the behest of McQuaid, as well as the international press attention which ensued, was the underlying cause of the Adoption Act in 1952 which legalized the lucrative international baby-trafficking market that the nuns had discovered. The reporter and writer, Mike Milotte, has estimated that The Church earned $30 to $50 million in today's money from the trade in babies. At 614, The Sacred Heart Sisters sent more babies abroad than any other institution. Father P.J. Reagan, the parish priest in Castlepollard (and preacher of many of the fire-and-brimstones sermons in Saint Joseph's chapel), was heavily involved with all the adoptions and particularly those to America. Father Reagan also ran Saint Claire's Adoption Society, which handled many of the adoptions from both Castlepollard and Saint Clare's Mother and Baby Home in nearby Stamullen, from where 130 babies were sent to the United States.

The first Irish Adoption Act was written in accordance with McQuaid's preferences and was referred back-and-forth to him on several separate occasions for his "comments." De Valera's government passed this act in 1952, which legally branded babies born outside wedlock as "illegitimate" human beings and second-class citizens. "Illegitimate" people were banned from joining the *Garda* (Irish police force) by the state and banned by the church from becoming priests without special papal dispensation. The act provides for the nuclear option of life-long closed adoption and sealed records. The situation remains unchanged in Ireland to this day, although the government did legally abolish the term "illegitimate" in 1987 and have also generously allowed adopted and illegitimate people to join the *Garda*.

From 1960 to 1973, in the three Sacred Heart-run Mother and Baby Homes, there were at least four trials of experimental and/or modified vaccines carried out by a state-employed Professor of Medicine on behalf of The Borris Wellcome Foundation (now a part of GlaxoSmithKline). These trials were carried out on control groups of babies up to 18-months-old who were held in the Mother and Baby Homes for up to a year and-a-half instead of being adopted. These trials were in direct contravention of the Constitution, the International CODEX guidelines, and the doctor's own Hippocratic oaths. The Nuremburg Code, issued during the trials of Nazi war criminals to prevent the type of experiments conducted by Nazi doctors (such as Josef Mengele) ever occurring again, was simply ignored by The Irish State. There was also a fifth trial in 1965 for which no one will take responsibility due to the fact that it was a disaster as the "test subjects" were accidentally adopted out shortly after the trial began. For thirteen years, the state and the GlaxoSmithKline precursor conspired to turn approximately 300 babies and young children into human lab rats in the three Sacred Heart Mother and Baby Homes and other institutions and orphanages. After the trials, the conspirators simply walked away. The babies were adopted out without their adoptive parents being informed of the trials or any form of monitoring or after-care, whatsoever. After the trials were finished, Borris-Wellcome/GlaxoSmithKline built a manufacturing facility in Ireland. The Sacred Heart Sisters continue to steadfastly deny that they had any knowledge that vaccine trials were being carried out in their three Mother and Baby Homes.

Six Castlepollard children are listed as test subjects in the Borris-Wellcome vaccine trials. During its thirty five years in operation, some 3,000 babies were born in Castlepollard, 2,500 were adopted out and another 500 died, although this figure could be higher. The babies are buried in a small angel's plot down a laneway, about quarter-of-a-mile from The Manor House. They were buried by the workman after dark, without coffins, names, or, in some cases, baptisms (which would have meant a huge amount to their mothers). The angel's plot is still bordered by two (of the original four) walls which are approximately 12-to-15 feet high.

The nuns ran down the numbers in Saint Peter's from 1969 through 1970 and finally sold the entire complex to the Midlands Health Board, the local name at that time for the government's Department of Health (now H.S.E.) in 1971.

In the early 1990s (at about the same time as the Irish public was learning about the clerical child abuse scandals and the horror of the industrial schools and the Magdalene Laundries), The Sacred Heart nuns arranged for money to be sent to have the Castlepollard angel's plot cleaned up. They also arranged for a small memorial stone to be erected. It is cheap limestone and the last word on the stone, cemetery, is misspelled as "cemetary" (with an "a" instead of an "e").

As far as is known, The Sisters burned almost every record when they vacated the property and there may be only four ledgers left as the sum total of the lives of the 6,000 mothers and babies who passed through Castlepollard (although some 15,000 files are now held by the Health Service Executive, it is unclear exactly what information they contain). Saint Peter's is now used as a residential care centre for adults with learning difficulties. It will be run down and closed over the course of 2013. No one knows what will happen to the buildings and property after that.

Between 1940 and 1965, in the oldest Mother and Baby Home (Saint Patrick's in Dublin and its sister hospital, Saint Kevin's) the bodies of at least 461 dead babies were "donated" for routine dissection practice by medical students and other research, to all the major medical teaching institutions in the state, including Trinity College Dublin, The College of Surgeons, and UCD medical school where the same Professor Meehan and Doctor (later Professor) Hillary, who conducted the vaccine trials, worked.

In both the vaccine trials and the "donation" of bodies, consent was neither sought from, nor granted by, either parent.

The McAleese Report showed almost one in every twenty-five Magdalene inmates were transferred there from a Mother and Baby Home.

From 1922 to 1952, all adoptions were technically long-term foster placements and only semi-legal (at best) and completely illegal (at worst). This group of *"de facto* adoptees" are in the worst legal position of all as they usually the victims of forged, fraudulent, or "missing" paperwork (many other people have also been the victims of illegal adoptions since 1952). A team of *Garda* and civil servants are needed to deal with this issue as a matter of urgency and criminal charges should be brought against any individual shown to be involved (whether for financial, ideological, or religious reasons).

Even though the heyday of the adoption industry has long

passed, the survivors are still dealing with the fallout and lifelong consequences. There are between fifty-and-sixty-thousand surviving adoptees in Ireland today, now mostly middle-aged or senior citizens. The women who lost their children to adoption are passing away without seeing or reconciling with their lost sons and daughters (or even knowing if they are dead or alive). The Internet, however, has allowed adoptees and their mothers to reunite without governmental or religious consent or mediation. Representative groups have formed, and are becoming more outraged by the day, as the full story of the Irish adoption machine is uncovered.

Adoptees in Ireland in 2013 still cannot obtain their original birth certificates or medical files even when their lives are at risk. The stories among the adoptee community concerning unknown and unknowable medical histories and the problems they cause are legion. Worse still is the situation of people who were never told they were adopted, or those who were illegally adopted, and have subsequently (and unknowingly) given false, misleading, and potentially-lethal medical histories to medical staff at intake. The state continues its cover up of adoption abuses and injustices by printing the legend "Birth Certificate" on what are, technically, extracts from the Adopted Children's Register. However, one positive development is that Irish adoptees have figured out how to collate the public records to match mothers of loss with their children. Detailed search and tracing guides are available online (as private tracing is 100% legal in Ireland).

The system of social workers meant to help adoptees and their mothers who wish to reunite, is chronically oversubscribed and slow. It is often indifferent and, at times, downright hostile. Some of the social workers employed by the state are now, or have in the past, been Sisters from the same Orders who were responsible for running the Mother and Baby Homes.

In August 2011, seven adoptees returned to Castlepollard where the present-day staff showed them around The Manor House (old convent), Saint Joseph's chapel (where they saw their baptism font), and the third floor of Saint Peter's hospital where they were born. They planted a tree in the angel's plot in memory of their lost brothers and sisters. They were the first adoptees to return as a group in the forty years after it had ceased operations. A year later, in August 2012, twenty-four attended. They planted flowers and left naming stones (inspired by an attempt to do the same at Bessborough where the Sacred Heart Sisters first granted, and then abruptly withdrew, their permission for a similar gathering without explanation). Another visit is planned for August the twenty-fifth 2013. Some Castlepollard adoptees and mothers have also formed small private groups on social networks.

From 1922 to the present, over 100,000 children have been born to single mothers who were effectively forced to hand over their babies for adoption because of the direct influence of The Church at all levels of Irish society. As proof that these adoptions were forced, one need only glance at what is happening in contemporary Ireland. Over the last generation, the number of single women choosing to have babies outside of marriage has shot up and now runs into tens-of-thousands each year. Yet the numbers of children put up for closed adoption to non-family members in Ireland is probably only between ten-to-twenty per year. In a civilised, relatively free society, women do not relinquish their babies.

Paul Redmond was born in a Castlepollard Mother & Baby home in 1964 and adopted 17 days later. After 30 years of pre-Internet research that involved meetings with three social workers, private detectives, solicitors, complaints and appeals, he finally connected with the growing Irish adoption-reform community. He returned to Castlepollard with several adoptees who held an informal memorial in the angels plot after visiting the main buildings. Shortly thereafter, he became an activist and co-founded "Adoption Rights Now," which now has a membership of over three hundred. He founded "The Castlepollard M&B Home Group," which annually tours the buildings, and also co-founded the international support and discussion group, "Adoptee Voices." He conducts research, writes reports, and has held meetings with the Archbishop of Dublin and Ireland's Minister for Children (among others). His submission is an extract from one of his reports (which can be viewed and downloaded online) which includes additional mortality rates.

The New Abolition:
Ending Adoption in Our Time

IN NO WAY SHOULD my color be regarded as a flaw. From the moment the Negro accepts the separation imposed by the European he has no further respite, and "is it not understandable that henceforth he will try to elevate himself to the white man's level? To elevate himself in the range of colors to which he attributes a kind of hierarchy?" We shall see that another solution is possible. It implies a restructuring of the world. – Frantz Fanon, *Black Skin, White Masks*

Introduction

Two years before I was born, Frantz Fanon's seminal work, *The Wretched of the Earth*, was published at the height of the Algerian War that France was waging against its rebellious colony. Fanon's text provides a framework for liberation from colonial subjugation and it describes the psychological and physical trauma inflicted by a foreign power upon a dominated populace. It further elucidates the functional role of the "native intellectual," the indigent who identifies with his colonizers. Fanon uses a striking passage to enlighten us concerning the mental makeup of those who acknowledge, accept, and finally assume the voice and narrative of the dominant culture. He states:

> "The intellectual who is Arab and French, or Nigerian and English, when he comes up against the need to take on two nationalities, chooses, if he wants to remain true to himself, the negation of one of these determinations. But most often, since they cannot or will not make a choice, such intellectuals gather together all the historical determining factors which have conditioned them and take up a fundamentally "universal standpoint."
>
> This is because the native intellectual has thrown himself greedily upon Western culture. *Like adopted children who only stop investigating the new family framework at the moment when a minimum nucleus of security crystallizes in their psyche*, the native intellectual will try to make European culture his own." [Emphasis mine.]

In comparing the colonized to the adopted child, Fanon makes an elliptical reference that greatly merits expansion. The implication here is that the adoptee also traverses the phases of being "colonized": coddled by the seeming safety of his new-found place, seduced by the imposed mythology of a dominant culture, and abetted by the willfully distanced memory of his generational past. Fanon thus provides a clear definition for what is often referred to within adoptee circles as "the fog" or "drinking the Kool-Aid": the acceptance of a fragile notion of security sustained by a false sense of self within an alien and alienating environment.

Given that adoption, like colonial oppression, is a function of a power differential determined by particular economic and political realities, Fanon's guide to liberation can equally be applied to the condition of the adopted child, subjugated both physically and psychologically within a foreign realm. As adoptees come to realize that their "minimum nucleus of security" is highly questionable not just within the family, but also within the world at large, the current normalizing analysis of the adoptee condition becomes an increasingly dubitable endeavor, especially when employing the tools, language, methods, and modes of the "colonial" system that engenders adoption in the first place.

Fanon's liberatory strategies of decolonizing our minds, as well as our sense of belonged-to place, provide a lifeline for the adoptee attempting to return to her land of birth or to assume her place in the culture of her adoption. Furthermore, they help us understand how our narratives mesh with others similarly displaced, including the immigrant-based families we are often adopted into. Finally, via these strategies, adoptees as well as their families, communities, and places of birth can attempt to find, at the very least, psychological solace from such a radical engagement, but more importantly they may discover a truly active role for themselves in this increasingly revolutionary world.

> "For poor people in many countries, Empire does not always appear in the form of cruise missiles and tanks, as it has in Iraq or Afghanistan or Vietnam. It appears in their lives in the very local avatars – losing their jobs, being sent unpayable electricity bills, having their water supply cut, being evicted from their homes and uprooted from their land. All this overseen by the repressive machinery of the state, the police, the army, the judiciary. It is a process of relentless impoverishment with which the poor are historically familiar. What Empire does is to further entrench and exacerbate existing inequalities."
> – Arundhati Roy, *Public Power in the Age of Empire*

A Deliberate Displacement

I returned sight-unseen to Lebanon, the country of my birth, in

September, 2004. Like many adoptees who make this journey back, I had in my head (and in my heart) a desire to know the culture, language, and place I had left at such an early age; a wish to literally fill in the blanks concerning aspects of my life that most take for granted: family, identity, ancestry. I've learned much in these past eight years, especially as I've engaged with other adoptees, many of whom have likewise returned to their own birthplaces. I have come to realize just how similar our stories are in fundamental ways and these common bonds have led to our activation concerning this issue.

As our activism has grown over this near decade, I have been greatly inspired by adoptees in South Korea, for just one example, who are attempting to shut down adoption in that country. Other source countries are following suit, and I am further heartened to see an expansion of this activism, here citing just a few examples: mothers in Guatemala, demanding the repatriation of their kidnapped children; in Argentina, demonstrating for an accounting of the infants born to the imprisoned and then disappeared; in Spain, investigating the stolen children of the Franco era and beyond; in Russia, criticizing the despicable treatment of their children exported abroad; in indigenous American Nations, parents reclaiming their stolen progeny. This list grows longer every day.

Such resistance does not pass without backlash. It is thus distressing to see renewed efforts to mediate adoption as a religious duty, or charitable act, as the front of this economic and political battle shifts to "virgin" countries and populations, in the biological version of neo-liberal plunder as described in such works as Naomi Klein's *The Shock Doctrine* or Samir Amin's *The Liberal Virus*. Nonetheless, I sense that we are reaching a crucial turning point, both for adoptees and their families, as well as for source countries and their communities, in which the very institution of adoption is challenged and critiqued not in terms of its reform, but openly and honestly in terms of its abolition.

I invoke this term fully aware of its weight as concerns the movement to abolish slavery and, to clarify this usage, I define adoption as follows:

> "Adoption is, in and of itself, a violence based in inequality. It is candy-coated, marketed, and packaged to seemingly concern families and children, but it is an economically and politically incentivized crime. It stems culturally and historically from the "peculiar institution" of Anglo-Saxon indentured servitude and not family creation. It is not universal and is not considered valid by most communal cultures. It is a treating of symptoms and not of disease. It is a negation of families and an annihilation of communities not imbued with any notion of humanity due to the adoptive culture's inscribed bias concerning race, class, and human relevancy."

From this standpoint, adoption is, in fact, similar to other present-day human displacements: slavery, trafficking, gentrification, immigration, land occupation, apartheid, and enforced statelessness. Our above list of those fighting for their children and families can equally be read as a rising tide of resistance against an economic and political war waged against them, with adoption now seen as a particularly focused weapon thereof. In the face of such violence, Fanon's words awaken us to our current "colonized" reality, force an examination of our relationship to, and positioning within, the places we might claim as our own and, in doing so, empower us with a common cause of resistance against the very economic and political roots that adoption stems from.

> "This is the certitude, always, of the authoritarian, the dogmatist, who knows what the popular classes know, and knows what they need even without talking to them. At the same time, what the popular classes already know, in function of their practice in the interwoven events of their everyday lives, is so "irrelevant," so "disarticulate," that it makes no sense to authoritarian persons. What makes sense to them is what comes from their readings, and what they write in their books and articles. It is what they already know

about the knowledge that seems basic and indispensable to them, and which, in the form of content, must be "deposited" in the "empty consciousness" of the popular classes."

— Paulo Freire, *Pedagogy of Hope*

The Negation of Identity

The nuclear family defines the basic unit of Anglo-Saxon economic and political systems and the rise of suburbia/exurbia in a post–World War II economic boom further equated "family" with economic arrival. Adhering to this "American Dream" required a very particular assimilation of those ascribing to this ideal, even when it ran counter to source countries and cultures. In immigrant communities, this transition often required generations; in this light, the adoptee becomes an idealized "new citizen," acculturated from the very start in the mores of a new and dominant culture.

This "benefit" runs both ways: Adopted children, as compared to immigrants, can thus be defined as stepping stones for the assimilation and advancement of the adoptive class, a leap-frogging of our progenitors who failed to "make it" in this type of globalized society. Projecting such a status on our adopters, we can thus be catalogued as "class markers," along with the house, car(s), major appliances, lawn, pool, summer home, and pedigree dog. Disturbingly enough, American Kennel Club certification of such animals contains more genealogical information than our own "birth" certificates.

This cataloguing is exemplified by the "Dear Birthmother" letters that litter the Internet. These atrocious human "fishing schemes" demonstrate to the subsisting mother-to-be how unfit she is to parent in the New Economy. The huge price of adoption, and the heinous exaltation of those who can pay such a fee, further manifests itself in fundraisers for adopter wannabes, as well as in T-shirts which gloatingly boast:

"Adoption: The New Pregnant," thus separating consumer purchase of a child from a more base procreation thereof.

Everything about the business transaction that is adoption – based on the Anglo-Saxon notion of children as property – attests to this concept, with its associated implications of ownership, transfer of title, racial authenticity, etc. This is represented by adoption brokers who, like their cohorts from the days of slavery, list the newborn (or not-yet-born) biological product for public viewing, including vital statistics such as gender, race, weight, health, and a price that repulsively varies based on the above parameters.

It should not surprise us then that we are given little sympathy when we speak out about losing our culture, language, or identity since many of our adoptive families, via generational erasure of an immigrant past, negated their own ethnicity to climb this same class ladder. This was done during times of social upheaval when those who resisted were violently put in their place, thus revealing the one valid path to take, now literally embodied in the economics of the adoption industry. To be told we were "chosen" or "lucky" is thus to emphatically berate our ingratitude concerning an instant economic arrival which often took generations for our adoptive families to accomplish.

In stark contrast, a sympathetic response to our question of identity is often worse than the outright dismissal thereof, especially when it involves the abysmal simulacrum of offensively named heritage camps. Similar to the historical segregation of immigrant minorities, these provide the very caricature of our ethnicity which, locally lived, is the source of the racist stereotypes directed against us, and that we are defenseless to counter in any significant way. Further to the point, they often reflect themes offensively removed from our originating nether-class communities, gleaned instead from the aristocratic, upper-class, or royal realm of our lands of birth. More insultingly still, they often employ references to culture completely disappeared or radically altered due to the onslaught of globalized cultural production.

The economic and political basis of such dictatorial indoctrination directed toward these "blank slates" and "impressionable slabs of clay" is evidenced in strikingly similar types of "children-gathering": the semi-adoption of "summer camps" for the very children victimized by imperial forays into countries such as Iraq, Afghanistan, Colombia, etc., as well as the cultural funding and "brain drain" scholarships from North America and Europe meant to win over "the hearts and minds" of those young people yearning to leave their home countries as much as we might hope to return to ours. The similarity here is not innocent nor coincidental, and we can see that the displacement of immigration and adoption are two different sides of the same imperial coin; and it is expected that we, too, must render unto Caesar.

> "Individualism is the first to disappear. The native intellectual has learned from his masters that the individual ought to express himself fully. The colonialist bourgeoisie had hammered into the natives mind the idea of a society of individuals where each person shuts himself up in his own subjectivity, and whose only wealth is individual thought."
> — Frantz Fanon, *The Wretched of the Earth*

An Honest Valuation of All Humanity

In defining adoption in this way, we must pursue this line of thinking to its logical conclusion especially as concerns its implications for the places we return to, also victims of various imperialist encroachments. As second-choice children and now second-class citizens, we are duty-bound to identify not with our acculturating class, but with our originating community wholly missing from this debate, in an effort to end our self-destructive oscillation and to find a true salvation in total immersion.

For what we describe is the economic and political system that we, adoptees, are aptly posed to challenge top to bottom.

To change adoption requires changing the system that spawned it and putting an end to its hegemonic reach. It is a natural next step for adoptees to thus fundamentally question adoption, deconstruct it, and eventually replace it with something much more socially conscious, holistic, and humane. This will not be accomplished from within the system as it currently exists, nor by conspiring with those who profit from it.

Extrapolating from Fanon, such change instead requires, among other things, a willful return to the local; a reawakening of true localized community-based culture; a move from monopolizing to cooperative models of industry, agriculture, and media; an honest valuation of all of humanity; a focus on family as an organic unit of a functional society and not of a consumptive economy; an examination of ethnic and cultural resistance within the trafficked experience; a prioritization of the communal over the individual; a focus on shared purpose over personal identity.

Such rethinking is not without work and effort. At its simplest, it means living as the rest of the world so lives and rejecting the luxuries and privileges that we currently confuse with personal and individual rights. At its most difficult, it is a complete decolonization of mind and place; a physical and psychological regrounding. The examples and precursors to follow here are many and varied, and their historic failure is more often a function of targeting from without. To consider such examples requires from us a shift in perception; a calling into question of that which we have been led to believe is the only possible way to exist framed along nationalistic, patriotic, and partisan class lines.

It is time for us to admit that in adoption can be found a great and horrific injustice and violence. But as is often the case, those who have suffered most from such violence are the ones who will most likely understand these words, are best primed en masse to right such wrongs, but for a variety of reasons (that, in and of themselves, support this thesis), are those most likely to never read or even hear them, much less act on them. And so we must become channelers on their behalf in an effort to reach them, to enjoin them, to bring true balance to this discussion, as well as an eventual rectification of what adoption has wrought.

> "The future of every man today has a relation of close dependency on the rest of the universe. That is why the colonial peoples must redouble their vigilance and their vigor. A new humanism can be achieved only at this price. The wolves must no longer find isolated lambs to prey upon."
> — Frantz Fanon, *Toward the African Revolution*

Positive Activism

To effectively communicate with those traditionally outside of the various failed metaphors used to describe the adoption equation — "triad," "constellation," and "mosaic" — we need delve into histories and narratives that are not found within the dominant discourse, ideally from the point of view of the subjects so excluded. For example, the derivations that led up to my adoption were many and complex. My adoptive father was working for a foreign oil company in Iran, naively unaware of the activation there of a society defying an imposed Shah after a British- and CIA-led coup toppled the democratically-appointed prime minister, Mohammad Mossadegh. Despite being an Islamic country, children from the nether classes were "adoptable," but they came with a hefty price tag that spat in the face of any concept of morality or ethics.

Lebanon was, for different purposes, likewise designed to be a capitalist haven from the moment it was carved out of a colonialist's map. It provided a palatable legal cover and an over-zealous brokerage for such transfers, and had started answering the demand for children from North America and Europe with a network of supply chains that stretched to the eastern hinterlands of the Beqa' Valley and Syria, as well as to the impoverished rural south, and into occupied Palestine. A random encounter in the Beirut airport started the verbal transaction that would later lead to a mountain of falsified documents that plagues me to this day. This, along with the support of a variety of governmental, religious, and diplomatic connections – along with a hefty price tag – allowed for my adoption and travel to the United States.

This historical pattern has been repeated an endless number of times around the world before (and since) then, with little protest from the class of adoptive parents taking advantage of this power differential in order to procure children for personal reasons that, as we see now, also serve a state/imperial function. Nearly fifty years after my birth, adoption is still fulfilling this fundamental role as a primary weapon of humanitarian imperialism, tactically erasing histories and cultures, breaking up families and communities, extracting wealth from the trafficking of human beings, and following up on, but also paving the way for, further repackaged and rebranded economic and political exploitation.

In those nascent days of the current phase of American empire, we might forgive those of our adoptive parents taken in by the likes of Pearl S. Buck and Harry Holt, these cheerleaders of empire who truly believed they were part of some Greater Manifest Destiny. In stark contrast, today's adoptive parents, in their globalized informational realm of existence, do not have this luxury of remove (nor may they feign ignorance of) the ponderous weight they throw around with their every purchase, vote, decision, and action. It is thus time to end this hideous charade and move to an honest discussion of what adoption truly represents as concerns those who suffer most for it, an acknowledgment of what the effect that decades of adoption will ultimately have on these populations, as well. We must endeavor to correct past actions and redirect energy and effort to one of positive activism on *their* behalf. In so doing, we will go much further to rebalance this greatly-skewed equation and debate, as well as to find answers to our own questions concerning our sense of self, identity, community, and place.

In 1963, **Daniel Ibn Zayd** was adopted at three-weeks-of-age from the *Crèche St. Vincent de Paul* in Beirut. Daniel's contribution is excerpted from a much larger work that attempts to provide a "people's history" of adoption, an analysis of current adoption practice and, finally, to prescribe an activist praxis that considers adoptees as activist agents alongside those who are equally displaced and dispossessed. The original article can be found on *The Dissident Voice*. Daniel currently lives and works in Beirut where he teaches art and illustration. In 2009, he founded the artists' collective, *Jamaa Al-Yad*. He has also helped to establish *Transracial Eyes*, a blog that joins a group of transracial and transnational adoptees. He is currently working on a book that examines the political and economic aspects of human trafficking, including adoption. You can find him at his eponymous website, *Daniel Ibn Zayd*.

I Can Never Forget

AFTERNOON. HOLIDAY. SUN IS SHINING. Normal people would spend this time with their families, but for those of us involved with Against Child Trafficking, this is not an option. Instead, we keep working and fighting (against all odds) for adoptee and children's rights. But none of us realized that the players involved would be so big or that we would find so little support for our work when we started. None of us thought that adoptees, and large parts of the adoption community, would fail to understand the crimes against humanity in order to develop workable solutions. To put it bluntly – the adoption community at large ensures that adoption will continue, business as usual.

Adoption (and, in particular, intercountry adoption) has become an open market for children, children who have been treated as a commodity and had their rights violated as citizens. I am an adoptee. I was a stolen child. I was sent to Germany, therefore, I was raised as a German. I was born in India, however, so I am also Indian. Like all human beings, adopted people have many facets to our identities. I am "Arun Dohle" now. That's what I have become due to adoption. That's what I am today. Some fifteen years ago, at the age of twenty-five, and like many adoptees, I just wanted to find out my roots, to learn about my home country, and to find my Indian mother. To be reunited was something I desired very deeply. I was stonewalled by my orphanage and various adoption experts who claimed to "protect" children. These organizations only protect themselves, but I was too young at the time to understand.

At the age of fourteen, I wanted to spend some time in India. Sadly, that was not possible, so I had to wait until after I finished school. It was impressive. I'll never forget the smell of the humid, thick air when I stepped off of the plane. The traffic was scary. I had never seen such a contrast between wealth and poverty as one can see in India. I spent about three months exploring the country.

Back in Germany, I studied business and, later, worked as a financial consultant. It was during that time that I met my future wife. All seemed well. I was successful in my career, but I wasn't really happy; there was something missing.

I decided that I would really try, at least once, to find my Indian mother. I thought that it might take one or two trips, but I could not imagine then the obstacles that I would face. I never imagined that my frequent trips to India would ultimately cause me to give up my job as a financial consultant.

In 2000, I started searching, in earnest, for my Indian family. My search coincided with the development of the Internet, therefore I turned to online forums. Soon, I realized that the adoption community (mostly adoptive parents and professional experts), were not supportive of my efforts. I was told that it was not possible and that it was against the law in India by the individuals who facilitated my adoption. *What? Meeting my mother is bad?* The agencies, the experts, even International Social Service were not willing to help me. I couldn't understand. I thought adoption was a good thing. *Why would everybody now deny me the right to know about my mother?* I dug deeper and learned that most of the adoptions in India were illegal and that there's a market for children. I learned of huge scandals, one of it is detailed in my report, titled "The Inside Story of an Adoption Scandal." We not only documented this scandal, but also fought it in court.

Adoptions from India started late in the 1960s and Europeans (mainly) adopted the children. In the 1980s, increasing numbers of children were sent to the United States. From 2002–to–2007, India sent approximately 5,600 children abroad. Families from the United States adopted approximately 2,400 of these children with India consistently ranking within the top ten countries of origin for Americans adopting children from overseas.

There is still no specific adoption law in India, but in 1984, the Supreme Court of India laid down detailed procedures for adoption after allegations of malpractice arose. These procedures form the basis for the Government's Guidelines on Adoption, enacted in 1989, 1995, and 2006. In 1993, India ratified the 1989 United Nations Convention on the Rights of the Child (UNCRC), which stipulates that intercountry adoptions are allowed only as a last resort if no other suitable manner of care is possible within the country and if no improper financial gain was made. On June 6, 2003, India ratified the Hague Convention on Adoption. Thus, in a sense, intercountry adoptions in India developed over a long period of time and can be considered well regulated, with multiple checks and balances in place.

However, no matter how well regulated one considers the Indian adoption system, allegations of corruption, kidnapping, and trafficking continue on a regular basis. For example, intercountry adoptions almost completely ceased in the state of Andhra Pradesh after it came to light that licensed adoption agencies indulged in the buying and selling of tribal infants. In 2005, it was discovered that in Tamil Nadu, children were kidnapped and sold to a licensed agency and adopted by foreigners. Additionally, adoptions in Delhi came to a temporary standstill in 2005 after the Department of Women and Child Development conducted an inquiry into the practices of licensed agencies and alleged that the agencies flouted the law by not putting abandoned children before the Child Welfare Committee, preferred foreigners to Indians, and failed to make adequate efforts to restore the children to their actual parents.

I couldn't believe it! *This was intercountry adoption?*

Despite all the time that I spent searching, I didn't make much headway. First, the orphanage lied to me and said that there were no records. However, it was frustratingly clear to me that the orphanage knew who my mother was and that they had no intention of revealing her identity to me.

In 2003, I was also told by a women and child rights activist that, according to Indian law, adoptees had a right to know about their parents. I had been misled by adoption experts and/or professionals for many years. Worse still, I had been *purposefully* misled.

Based on this new knowledge, I started a court case against my orphanage which took a lot of time and cost me my job.

Today I also feel that the pain involved with the search for my mother, and the amount of time and money I spent on it, took a toll on my own family. Sometimes, I wish I could be just like any other father and husband and not be affected by such a life story. At the same time, I hoped that no adoptee would ever be forced to suffer like I had. I tried to share my knowledge and contacts with other adopted people. Working with other adoptees, it became more and more clear that we are all part of a lucrative business. *Strange.*

In 2005, I took up real casework. With my Indian friends, we started assisting Indian families whose children were kidnapped for intercountry adoption. Initially, I thought that if I informed the adoption agency of the fact that the children were kidnapped that they, at least, would establish contact with the Indian families to correct the injustices. *Damn, was I wrong!*

In 2007, the kidnapping cases were highly publicized in the Dutch media. It became a huge scandal after the Dutch government's investigations started. Soon, I figured out that they were going to be shallow (and I was right). To date, the Dutch government pretends not to know anything about what has actually transpired in India. Meiling, the agency, is still in operation today. They received a slap on the wrist, but that was all.

My investigations led me to a legalized child marketplace. Regulating intercountry adoption means defining exact procedures about how to relinquish children, how to declare children officially "abandoned," and putting caps on the length of time dedicated to finding local care solutions. Regulating intercountry adoption also means the courts will blindly validate adoptions and complete the Hague certificate after the fact with the central authority. This creates a watertight system that protects clients, but leaves actual parents powerless without any recourse.

In the receiving countries, the Indian regulation misleads prospective adopters. Their impression is that, since adoptions are well regulated (with checks and balances in place), the exported children are indeed "orphans" (with both parents being deceased) and that the best solution to the problem is for them to be adopted by foreigners. Media exposure may shake this confidence momentarily, but the confidence quickly returns after experts confirm the "legality" of the procedures.

The rules developed under the guise of the Hague Convention do not prevent abuses, but instead prevent them from being seen. They mystify and hide the inherent injustice behind a legalized smokescreen. The result is the demand-driven creation of "legal orphans" who, according to their paperwork, could not be cared for in their own countries. The reality is that India could easily care for the 700 to 1,000 children sent abroad annually. This is a matter of political choice.

I met Roelie Post, a civil servant of the European Commission, in 2007 in the aftermath of the Dutch/India scandal just after she had released a book called, *Romania for Export Only: The Untold Story of the Romanian Orphans*. She explained that the heart of the matter is the fact that children have rights in their own country as outlined in the United Nations Convention for the Rights of the Child as originally intended and properly interpreted. Intercountry adoption as it has been practiced (and even enforced by adoption facilitators) is a violation of the children's rights, which can be considered child trafficking. In her article "The Perverse Effects of the Hague Adoption Convention," she explains how "parents are often tricked into relinquishing their children without understanding the full concept of adoption (thinking the children will come back). And while old markets [for adoptable children] close," her paper explains, "the travelling circus of adoption agencies moves on and a new market is evolving in Africa. Particularly, Ethiopia has seen an exponential growth over the last years."

I spoke with Roelie Post every evening for three full months, asking her again and again the same questions regarding the UN Convention on the Rights of the Child. I just couldn´t believe that the core of the adoption issue could be that simple. Of course I knew about the UNCRC. I had read the Hague Adoption Convention and, since all the so-called experts recommended implementation of the HAC as a solution to the trafficking mess, I just couldn't understand the significance of the difference between these two conventions.

The UNCRC is a very comprehensive treaty and its articles are indivisible. It's clear that children should be cared for within close proximity to their actual families. Having lost my identity, culture, and language, I slowly realized that this was all vital during my personal journey for my identity.

In a nutshell, she explained to me that the Hague Adoption Convention tries to overwrite the UNCRC and, by doing so, changes the meaning of Article 21b and 20c. Foster care, institutional care (also quality residential care), and any other suitable manners of care are not considered by the Hague Adoption Convention as "child protection" measures. Skipping those options greatly benefits adoption agencies.

Families and mothers have a right to greater assistance (for example, "family preservation"), not just limited assistance.

Adoption, as such, should be considered the last resort (if at all) and is a very drastic measure, changing the identity of the child completely and cutting ties to the child's family forever. Most countries don't really even understand the concept of (Western) adoption. Even in my adoptive country of Germany, the practice of intercountry adoption isn't really considered a child-protective measure where children are shipped to a foreign land.

This took me more than three months to fully understand. Sometimes, the simple things are the most difficult ones to grasp. All my friends, considered experts within the field of adoption, were promoting the Hague Convention.

Roelie explained that, in her work for the European Commission, she assisted Romania in reform along the lines of the UNCRC but, due to the adoption lobby/mafia, it was necessary to set up an independent panel to ensure that the new Romanian legislation was in line with the UNCRC.

And it was. The panel also held that adoption is not a child-protective measure...

When I met Roelie in 2007, she had just released her book, *Romania: For Export Only*, a diary detailing her lobbying efforts that worked to prevent Romania, like all old European-Union member states, from exporting their children. In pursuance of the Secretary General of the European Commission, Roelie set up her own Non-Government Organization (Against Child Trafficking) in 2007 and provided a lot of her own funding for ACT's work. Because of it, we have fought numerous cases, including one against Madonna's second adoption from Malawi.

Overall, the current adoption system actively makes an inordinately high number of children available for adoption. After investigating how children are obtained for adoption, it was clear to me that Roelie's position on children's rights was correct. The ratification of the Hague Convention has demonstrated no guarantee against child trafficking (Romania was the first country to ratify it and India has had a Hague-compliant system since 1995).

Local child protection policies exist on paper, but are not implemented, while the intercountry adoption market is increasingly more in control of local child protection. The adoption process is riddled with fraud and other criminal activities. Parents are officially declared "dead" (when, in fact, they are not), dates of birth are falsified, and this false information is provided to the courts. But, most importantly: The demand-driven intercountry adoption process is breaking up families who could be helped by a fraction of the money associated with intercountry adoption.

Here is a summary of one of ACT's investigations: In the beginning of 2008, we started communication with the Dutch adoption agency, *Wereldkinderen*. We began working together on searches and the right to know ones roots in India. Also, we cooperated in field research in Ethiopia and talked with families who had been left behind. The objective was to find out whether their representatives had engaged in criminal activity. Another objective was to find out whether the actual family members had really understood the full consequences of the relinquishment of their child for (intercountry) adoption, meaning the permanent termination of all legal and social ties with their child.

While traveling through Ethiopia, foreign adoption agencies were omnipresent (as the big US agencies pump significant amounts of money into the country). Holt, for example, has overtaken a governmental health center in Shinchicho, giving it access to the 250,000 people living in this region. Children's Home Society and Family Services both operate a Mother and Child Health Center. Christian World Adoption currently invests in a whole village for children and adjacent accommodations for adoptive parents.

It is clear that Ethiopian family services are becoming increasingly dependent on funding from foreign adoption agencies risking that, in "return," more and more children will need to be made available for intercountry adoption. Oftentimes, families do not receive any post-adoption information, despite the fact that it had specifically been promised to them.

> "In the Constitution of Ethiopian Law, Article 36 states that every child has a right: To life; (b) To a name and nationality; (c) To know and be cared for by his or her parents or legal guardians; (d) Not to be subject to exploitative practices..."

The Ethiopian Guidelines clearly incorporate the principals of the UNCRC. Therefore, before considering intercountry adoption, other care options have to be truly and actively sought.

Under Ethiopian law, the bond with the actual family should continue to exist after adoption. The Ethiopian guidelines stipulate that the actual family has the right to be updated about the wellbeing of their child (or children).

This "right" is, devastatingly, not enforced. This promise constitutes a misrepresentation of the reality that Ethiopian families face and a grave deception. It is questionable, then, if the actual families would have then consented to the adoption if they had been fully informed about the fact that they would not be given post-adoption reports on their children. Little-to-no effort is made to retain any child within its own family, community, or through other in-country care options.

The Ethiopian social and legal concept of adoption seriously differs from the Western/European version. Ethiopian families expect their adopted children to care for the family in the future. Under Ethiopian law, the actual family has a right to remain intact. In general, a lack of understanding of the Western concept of adoption was evident. Most parents or relatives expected updates about the adopted children and also expected their children to return once he, or she, turned eighteen. By then, however, the child has been so indoctrinated into their adoptive culture that they rarely think to return to help the family that they assumed had abandoned them.

Based on the 2009 findings from scientific research done at Addis Ababa University on Ethiopian parents who have relinquished their children for intercountry adoption, it was concluded that Ethiopian parents are challenged with moderate-to-severe levels of depression after relinquishing their children. To overcome their losses, their only coping strategies have been to pray and to talk to friends. The findings are reason for serious concern. In most cases, there was no proper counseling and no other support was offered to keep the family together. Also, no efforts were made to find a suitable manner of care for the children in Ethiopia. In fact, intercountry adoption was (and is) used as a *first option*, rather than as a last resort. In a number of cases, the information in the adoption file and on the Court Order was incorrect (as in the cases of parents being declared "dead" when they were, in fact, very much alive). Also some of the children's birthdates were erroneous.

The researched cases paint a bleak picture of the reality of Ethiopian adoption. It appears that there is a system for collecting children from villages. Orphanages send their busses. Child recruiters are paid monthly salaries. These recruiters are also active in health centers and other places where families go for help. While investigating, it felt inappropriate and too hurtful for me to confront the Ethiopian families with the full reality of intercountry adoption, i.e., that they had permanently lost all ties with their child (or children). When I returned home from my investigation, we wrote the "Fruits of Ethiopia" report which asked the question: Is intercountry adoption really for the protection of the child? Or is it simply the "harvesting" of children?

Intercountry adoption from Ethiopia has increased exponentially in recent years. However, as countries like Romania, Guatemala, Cambodia, Nepal and Vietnam have stopped supplying children to the global market, this has resulted in an influx of adoption agencies to Ethiopia. While there are no formal statistics available, it is estimated that adoptions increased from just a few hundred to more than four thousand in a span of a few years. More than 70 foreign adoption agencies are registered by the Ministry for Women; some of these are umbrellas for other (US) agencies. In Austria and Canada, Ethiopian adoptions have made headlines as adopted children who were declared "orphans" were proven to have living parents and/or other relatives, the ages of some children were incorrect (children were much older than officially reported), and others had hidden health issues.

I will never forget the mothers and fathers who have lost their children to intercountry adoption. Their sorrow and grief still haunts me to this day. My final wish is for justice for all families who have been destroyed by adoption.

Do you have a child? Can you imagine if your child were to be "stolen" from you and sent to another country to be adopted? Can you believe that the current adoption system legalizes such practices? That your child now has a new name, a new identity, and a new family? That you have NO rights anymore? That you can never see your child again? That no authority is helping you? That the agencies who were involved in these crimes are still allowed to operate? Is this in the best interest of your child?

In 2001, **Arun Dohle** started looking for his mother in India. While in India, he met with children's and women's rights activists, other adoptees, and adoptive parents. He soon realized that his adoption papers were incorrect. Together with other Indian activists, Arun started doing field research and discovered several cases where children were either blatantly kidnapped or sent by their parents for temporary care into a children's home, but then sent abroad without their knowledge or consent. One case was picked up by a major television programme. A documentary filmmaker went to India with Arun and the scandal was brought out in the Netherlands. Since then, Arun has worked on child trafficking field casework in Malawi, Ethiopia, and India, resulting in several investigative reports. He is cofounder of Against Child Trafficking and is regularly quoted by journalists worldwide.

Against Child Trafficking is a Brussels-based children's rights organization, registered in The Netherlands.

ACT promotes the proper implementation and original intent of the UN Convention on the Rights of the Child (UNCRC) that first and foremost gives children the right to be cared for by their parents. It is the responsibility of the State to support families and communities in the upbringing of their children. Intercountry adoption may only be considered if there is no way at all to bring up a child in-country (and that includes foster and residential care). All efforts should be made to keep families together.

In the last fifty years, an adoption industry has been developing that serves the growing demand for children in the Western world – an industry in which huge sums of money are involved. Children are sold (these payments are reclassified as "adoption fees") mainly through licensed and accredited adoption agencies regulated by adoption laws.

ACT considers this a demand-driven market for children, which should be labeled as child trafficking and stopped. Children have rights. Children should not be commodities.

The United States and Somalia are the only countries in the world who have not ratified with the United Nations Convention for the Rights of the Child (UNCRC).

There are no laws in the United States to protect children against adoption trafficking.

In the effort to protect unsuspecting and vulnerable families worldwide, **Against Child Trafficking USA** was formed to educate the public on the crisis of adoption trafficking.

The Definition of Human Trafficking according to the United Nations Office of Drugs and Crime (UNODC):

"Article 3, Paragraph (a) of the Protocol to Prevent, Suppress and Punish Trafficking in Persons defines Trafficking in Persons as the Recruitment, Transportation, Transfer, Harbouring or Receipt of persons, By means of Threat/Force, Coercion, Abduction, Fraud, Deception, Abuse of Power or of a position of vulnerability, giving or receiving of payments or benefits to achieve the consent of a person having control over another person, for the purpose of exploitation."

Exploitation: "The practice of taking selfish or unfair advantage of a person or situation, usually for personal gain."

How adoption trafficking might look today: African (or vulnerable) parents are recruited from rural areas and deceptively told that their children will receive an education and/or have a "better life" in the West by honest-looking "authority" figures who appear to be ethical and actively working in the children's "best interest."

Upon hearing some potentially good news – which can seem like a scholarship to some families – the vulnerable and unsuspecting parents give consent, believing that they will one day see their child (or children) again. They do not know that their children's identity will be altered and then he, or she, will be processed and transferred overseas for intercountry adoption under the guise of being "orphans."

Sadly, the children are taken from their parents, harboured in orphanages and given fraudulent paperwork that leaves the impression that they are without families or have been abandoned. The parents are not invited into any of the care facilities, boarding schools, hostels, nurseries, or community centers which are advertised as "orphanages" in the West. In fact, poverty-stricken parents are directed to leave the premises and some children are then transferred to prevent further contact.

After the retail agency receives payment from prospective couples via a service fee (some have charged up to $75,000 per child depending on race and country of origin), and then pays the orphanage partner, the children are collected and flown overseas to the foreign clients. Some children have been abducted from China or India, where at least 60,000 children are reported missing in each country every year.

By the time the adopted children reach adulthood and decide to look for their families, it is too late. They are refused access to adoption documents and given incomplete information. Many facilitators will claim that the records have been destroyed and some facilitators cannot be found (or are no longer in business).

Good news! Great gains have been made globally. With knowledge comes power. Adopted people and their families have been validated and are often reunited. And, because of worldwide connections and websites, like *Adoptionland.org*, prospective couples can be much better informed.

What you can do: Join the dialogue on Facebook at "Adoption Truth and Transparency Worldwide Network" or gift copies of *Adoptionland* to friends and educational organizations. Assistance with fundraising or sharing news about efforts to stop adoption trafficking are always welcome.

We can make a difference in the lives of fellow human beings. By being aware and providing education, we can prevent at-risk, rural, and native parents from being unnecessarily separated from their most precious resources: *their children.*

Cover Art

"It Never Should Have Been Like This"

Darius Morrison is a fine-art printmaker and musician. He uses autobiographic images to explore the complex intersections of his queer, FTM-transgendered, and Korean-adoptee identities. He is currently an artist member with IDEA Odyssey Gallery, a visual arts collective promoting cultural diversity, community, and economic development in Seattle's International District. He is an active member of the Pacific Northwest's Queer People of Color communities. He is also the guitarist for the art-rock band, Nation of Two.

"Birthmothers" are a social construction. The term was devised by adoption professionals to reduce a natural mother to that of a biological function. This term marginalizes mothers and creates a role for them in society which does not allow them to fully embrace their lived experience as a mother, implying instead that the sacred bond of mother and child ends at birth and that her role is secondary to other mothers in society.

– Valerie Andrews, Executive Director of Origins Canada